Berlitz®

D0676239

THAILAND

- A ✓ in the text denotes a highly recommended sight
- A complete A–Z of practical information starts on p.115
- Extensive mapping throughout: on cover flaps and in text

Printed in Switzerland by Weber SA, Bienne - October 1997

3rd edition

Although we make every effort to ensure the accuracy of the information in this guide, changes do occur. If you have any new information, suggestions or corrections to contribute, we would like to hear from you. Please write to Berlitz Publishing at the above address.

Text:	Ben Davies
Editors:	Jane Middleton, Donald Greig
Layout:	Cristina Fino Silva
Photography:	Ben Davies
Cartography:	Falk-Verlag, Hamburg
Thanks to:	the Tourist Authority of Thailand (TAT) for their invaluable assistance in the preparation of this guide.

Cover photograph: Wat Benchamabophit, Bangkok
                     © Tony Stone Worldwide

CONTENTS

Thailand and the Thais

Thailand infuses all the colour and excitement of the Far East with its own particular charm. From its glittering temples and smiling people to palm-lined beaches and shady hideaways, it has more to offer than just about any other destination in the world. Colourful markets, villages on stilts, and exotic national parks where elephants run wild are among its attractions; even the monolithic new cities are filled with an irresistible blend of Western and Oriental allure.

Bigger than Spain, but a bit smaller than France, Thailand is more than spacious enough to be home to all the scenery you could imagine. Its tallest peak, near Chiang Mai in the north, is a respectable height of about 2,590m (8,500ft). On the central plain around Bangkok, however, the landscape of paddy fields, rivers, and canals is as flat and green as a billiard table. Over 70 percent of the population is involved in rice farming, not to mention several million water buffalo, too.

Thailand's climate, which is officially classified as tropical monsoon, is best enjoyed from November to February, when the relatively cool, dry air rolls down from China to the north, reducing Bangkok's temperatures from scorching to merely hot. In the northern hills, you might even find yourself wanting a sweater after sundown. Between May and October, the south-west monsoon alternates deluges with rainbows.

No matter when you reach Bangkok, the main commercial and political centre, you should be ready for heat, pollution and sheer chaos. This is a place that was once known as the Venice of the East, with canals criss-crossing the somnolent, riverine streets. Nowadays, although the old way of life still exists along the waterways, you are more likely to find massive traffic jams and high-rise buildings.

Estimates of the population of Bangkok stand at around 8 million people, or 12 percent **5** of the entire country – a figure that continues to grow in leaps and bounds – and the city contains over one million cars and 11 thousand restaurants. Even here, however, amidst all the chaos, there are things that are uniquely Thai, from chanting Buddhist monks and bustling marketplaces, to spirit houses heaped with colourful orchids and lotus blossom.

Over 90 percent of the population is Buddhist, and both the religion and philosophy of Buddhism permeate all facets of national life. Founded in India, Buddhism first came to Thailand in 303 BC, when it thrived as the religion of kings

There is a little piece of sand for everybody in Phuket, the pearl of Thailand's tourist industry and the largest island in the kingdom.

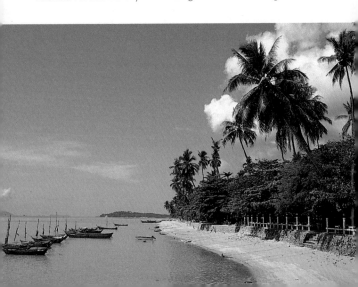

and as a unifier of the people. To see Buddhism in practice today, you will not have to go very far. At dawn, even in the capital, you will see monks on the early-morning alms round. Those lucky enough to be present at an ordination ceremony in a temple witness the most magnificent sight of all: saffron-robed novices being carried high above the shoulders of friends and family.

Monks are not the only outward sign of the religion that, along with the monarchy, has given strength and continuity to the kingdom. Great temples offered to Buddha can be seen everywhere; the Grand Palace or the Wat Arun shouldn't be missed in Bangkok, or, further afield, the magnificent ruins of Sukhothai or Ayutthaya.

If you prefer more natural attractions, head for one of the vast national parks, which now constitute a huge 34,500sq km (12,700sq miles) of Thailand. Of particular note is Khao Yai park because of its birdlife and waterfalls. Iridescent kingfishers and orange-breasted, red-headed trogons flit beneath the shade of leafy canopies. Gibbons and flying squirrels, elephants, black bears and tigers dwell in these vast stretches of dense evergreen. The bird life is prolific and you might catch a glimpse of any one of over 900 different species. Orchids grow in abundance, and there is a multitude of butterflies.

Further south, if you want underwater adventure, cruise to beautiful Ko Phi Phi, or explore the long, lazy beaches at famous Phuket and Ko Samui.

*F*ood for thought? A pensive moment for a local girl, tucking into a guava-like farang fruit.

7

However, it is the people, even more so than the sights and scenery, who often afford the most memorable experiences. From friendly northerners to the rice farmers in the central plains, the philosophy underlying every aspect of life is simply *mai pen rai* (literally 'no worries'). Such a relaxed attitude has its roots partly in Thailand's history, for unlike almost all the rest of South East Asia, Thailand was never subject to European power, so historical resentment towards foreigners has never featured. Thailand translates as 'Land of the Free', and the Thai people take pride in their past and in their constitutional monarchy, both of which are significant to uniting the country.

More unspoilt are the arid plains of Isaan in the north east – or alternatively, trek among the hill people of the Golden Triangle up north, where poppies have earned it a reputation as one of the world's largest opium-producing regions.

Don't miss the opportunity of a trip on the Mekong either. One of the world's great rivers, it runs down from Tibet, irrigating the rice fields in the north of Thailand, before it empties out in the Nam Khong Delta of South Vietnam.

The figures of one census put the population of Thailand at 55 million, over 70 percent of which inhabit the countryside. Not everyone is of pure Thai stock, and it is estimated that as many as 3 million residents are descendants of migrants from Burma, Laos, and Cambodia, who came to Thailand hundreds of years ago.

Economically, the Thais are rapidly emerging as a major industrial nation to join the so-called 'tigers' of Korea, Hong Kong, Singapore and Taiwan. Although 60 percent of the population still farm the land, producing over 22 million tons of rice each year and enabling Thailand to remain the world's chief exporter of tinned pineapple, the country also exports significant volumes of textiles, electronics and jewellery.

Not that work is allowed to interfere with play. Thais love the good things in life, a fact that is clear from their enjoyment of Thai food, which is on a par with French and Chinese

Honoured with flowers at Wat Phra Kaeo (left). Saffron-robed monks gather at dawn for their alms round at the Marble Temple.

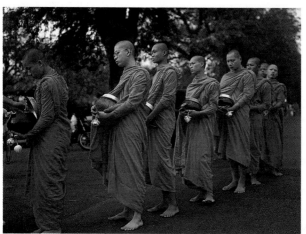

as one of the world's classic cuisines. Typical flavours and tastes are spicy, sour, hot and sweet, and the success of these dishes often relies on delightful contrasts which ensure the palate never becomes jaded. Delicacies such as prawns in coconut, or succulent chicken

Picking rice in the paddies of the central plains can occupy a whole life time.

wrapped in a banana leaf, take their place amongst an array of culinary specialities. Indeed, it would probably be possible to enjoy a different type of dish every day of your visit and still leave plenty untasted.

Just the thing to work up an appetite for feasting is a visit to the shops and markets, for Thailand is one of South East Asia's finest shopping destinations. Keep an eye open in the markets for beautifully woven baskets, or for the silk that is famous worldwide, due to its quality. If you're in the north, go in search of colourful umbrellas – you can watch while they're being painted – and wherever you are, don't overlook traditional wooden carvings (but don't be taken in by more modern imitations either, which are usually less attractive, and not always cheaper).

Thailand is uniquely positioned to satisfy the wishes of all its visitors. By the time you leave you may not understand, but you will certainly appreciate the mystery and beauty of one of the most fascinating countries of South East Asia.

A Brief History

Recent archaeological finds in north-east Thailand are turning traditional ideas on their head. Relics discovered in the village of Ban Chiang and dating back over 5,000 years are still being studied, but seem to prove that Thailand was home to one of the first Bronze Age civilizations in the world, pre-dating that of China.

What happened to the pre-historic people is not known. As for the Thais, it is probable that they did not reach the area until the 11th or 12th century. According to anthropologists, they then spread south across vast areas of the fertile Chao Phya valley, at the same time displacing both the Mons and Khmers. Around 1259 AD, the kingdom of Lan Na (Land of a Million Rice Fields) was established in what is now northern Thailand. Chiang Rai was chosen as capital to start with, but when King Mengrai spotted five white mice, two white sambars, and two white barking deer together on the banks of the Ping River, he relocated the capital to Chiang Mai.

Mengrai ruled prosperously until the age of 80, when he was struck by lightning. (Later kings died in even more surprising ways, like King Kamphoo, whose brief reign ended in 1345 when he was devoured by a crocodile. In more recent times, in 1946, Rama VIII, the brother of the present king of Thailand, was found shot dead in bed. The mystery around his death remains unsolved.)

Dawn of Happiness

The first great chapter of Thai history began with King Ramkamhaeng the Great, the ruler of Sukhothai (founded at some time in the 1230s) from about 1280 to 1317. Ramkamhaeng – who was renowned for legendary exploits on elephants – managed to nurture a powerful kingdom and a thriving haven for the arts. In its heyday, the kingdom stretched from Lampang in the north of Thailand to Vientiane, now part of Laos, and south towards the Malay Peninsula. Many scholars say **11** that the first Thai alphabet derives from this period. Sukhothai contributed some of the finest examples of Thai sculpture in history, many of which can still be viewed in parts of the old city today.

However, after the death of King Ramkamhaeng, the kingdom's power declined. By the 15th century the city was little more than a provincial town, and shortly afterwards it was abandoned altogether.

Ayutthaya

Sukhothai's downfall cleared the way for what was to be an even greater kingdom. Established in 1350, Ayutthaya continued for over 400 years and earned a place as one of the East's greatest civilizations.

Under King U-Thong and a succession of legendary monarchs, the kingdom expanded rapidly. Towards the end of the 14th century, the Khmers were driven out of vast areas of central and northern Thailand, and the people of Sukhothai were finally vanquished. In 1431 the capital at Angkor in Cambodia

was sacked, and Ayutthaya's pre-eminence was established beyond question.

Ayutthaya became a centre for trade between China, India and Europe, in which teak and spices were bartered for gold and cannon which the Siamese pulled behind their elephants.

In spite of the loss of several kings – who were either cudgelled to death or poisoned – the people of Ayutthaya were, by all accounts, a happy lot, 'much given to pleasure and ryot' according to the observations of one 17th-century traveller. Opium was in abundant supply, and cohabitation and wife-swapping found enthusiastic supporters.

Most foreigners who came to Ayutthaya during the 17th century were impressed by the sheer size and opulence of the Siamese capital. Directors of the East India Company compared it favourably with London, estimating its population to be anything from 300,000 to 1 million. With palaces, canals and temples, the city acquired a justified reputation of being the most beautiful in Asia.

European influence reached its zenith during the reign of King Narai (1657-88), when the courts of Siam were visited by ambassadors from as far as the court of Louis XIV, along with explorers, zealous Jesuit missionaries, and traders. One Greek adventurer, named Geraki Constantine Phaulkon, was

The chedis of Wat Phra Si Sanphet were once part of a group of buildings at the King's Palace; they are amongst the finest in Ayutthaya.

Kings Rule OK

When it came to rhetorical flourishes, the monarchs of Ayutthaya in the 17th century took the biscuit. Any mortal who was so bold as to address the king was obliged to start as follows: 'High and mighty Lord of me thy slave, I desire to take thy royal word and put it in my brain and on the top of my head.' Those that failed to follow this code of conduct were summarily chastised with bamboos. Others were buried alive in the cement walls surrounding the city.

Between the 15th and 18th centuries, the Thais fought innumerable battles against the neighbouring Burmese. A consequence of this was the conflict of April 1767, when after a 14-month siege, the Burmese succeeded in capturing Ayutthaya. They pillaged the city and vandalized every aspect of Thai culture and art. The sack of Ayutthaya, a great tragedy in Thai history, still casts a shadow over the national consciousness of the Thai people.

One survivor, a young general from Tak province, rallied the remnants of the Thai army and managed to expel the Burmese garrison. Ayutthaya had been almost totally destroyed, however, so Taksin – as he was known – founded a new capital at Thon Buri, directly across the river from what has since become Bangkok. Though his father was actually Chinese – and a commoner at that – Taksin was crowned king of Thailand. He ruled until 1782, at which point he was dethroned on the grounds of madness and ceremoniously executed with a club of scented sandalwood.

even appointed the king's first minister, and acted as the principal go-between when diplomatic exchanges were held.

Such promotion inevitably sparked jealousy, however, and shortly before the king died in 1688, Phaulkon was executed after being arrested at the time of a bloody revolt. After this incident, Thailand had almost no contact with the West for the following 150 years.

From Thon Buri to Bangkok

With the death of Taksin, there rose to power the first king of the Chakris dynasty, the greatest in Thai history, which still sits on the throne today.

Rama I immediately moved his capital from Thon Buri to Bangkok on the east bank of the river, saying that the new city would be larger and easier to defend. He then went on to defeat a number of marauding Burmese expeditions.

His son, Rama II, devoted himself to preserving Thai literature, and produced a classic version of the Thai *Ramayana* or *Ramakien*, the epic Sanskrit poem. He also re-established

The mythical naga snake that raised Buddha to heaven guards the entrance to temples.

relations with the West, and still found time to sire 73 children by 38 mothers.

Although no less influential, Rama III (1824-51) is largely overlooked by historians. As a devout Buddhist he built some of Bangkok's finest temples, including Wat Arun and parts of Wat Pho. He also went on to introduce Western medicine to his country – including small-pox vaccinations – as well as arranging for American missionaries to visit, one of whom brought the first printing press with Thai type.

The King and I

The most renowned of all the early monarchs is, lamentably, better known for his excessive libido than his actual achievements. King Mongkut, a Buddhist monk for 27 years, took 35 wives by whom he had 83 children. He was depicted as a

A serene statue of Buddha in Ayutthaya, once said to be the most beautiful city in Asia.

cruel, frivolous despot in the memoirs of court tutor Anna Leonowens, which later provided the basis for the film *The King and I*. This reputation has saddened the Thais, who still worship Mongkut as one of the greatest and most progressive monarchs. Not only was he a man of considerable sophistication, he was also better educated than the kings of Europe. He could speak seven foreign languages, including Latin and English, and was an expert in astronomy. It was during his reign that commoners were allowed for the first time to set eyes on the King of Siam, waterways and roads were built, and laws set down to improve rights for women and children.

Mongkut was succeeded by Rama V, who became known as Chulalongkorn, or Lord of the White Elephant, and was one of the most popular and enlightened of all the kings. During his 42-year reign, he abolished slavery and established a schooling system, the first post office and a national library. He led his country literally as well as symbolically **17** into the 20th century – and is still remembered with considerable affection today.

The World Wars

The effect of World War I was to propel Thailand out of isolation. In 1917, King Vajiravudh (Rama VI) dispatched troops to France to support the Allied cause. A likely explanation for his sympathies is that he was Cambridge educated and had served for a time in the British army. Once the war was over, Siam became a member of the League of Nations.

One legacy of Rama VI was surnames for the Thai people. Prior to the war, family names were not used in Siam, but the king decreed that all his subjects adopt one. Women were encouraged to grow their hair long like Western women and even football was introduced, with a Royal team.

The genteel world of Siam was rocked once more in 1932, when a group of army officers staged a bloodless revolution which brought the monarchy's absolute supremacy to an end.

The authorities of Siam (by then renamed Thailand) signed friendship agreements with the Japanese in 1940. The following year, the Japanese invaded Thailand and soon afterwards the Thais, seeing resistance as hopeless, entered World War II on the side of the Axis. Despite the fact that Thailand was on the losing side, it was later able to join the United Nations due to a legal loophole in the original declaration of war.

Since 1932, continual political turbulence has beset Thailand. The country has endured 17 coups, while over 31 prime ministers have been appointed, none of whom has lasted a full term. Ironically though, Thailand is deemed one of the most stable countries in a part of the world which until recently was regarded as extremely volatile. It sided with America during the Vietnam War, and throughout its history it has remained resolutely anti-communist and pro-monarchy.

Even now, however, the balance is uncertain. In May 1992 more than 100 pro-democracy demonstrators were either shot

Coup de Grace

Of all the attempted military coups in Thailand (17 in total), that which took place in 1950 must be recorded as one of the most bizarre. In May of that year, Prime Minister Phibul Song-khram was forced at gunpoint on to a naval ship moored in the Chao Phya River. Negotiations failed to break the deadlock, and loyal forces launched an air and ground attack on the vessel, but fearing for the safety of their respected hostage, Phibul's captors helped him to swim to shore. Once there he telephoned headquarters, was picked up and returned to power intact.

*P*omp, circumstance and a stiff salute – changing the guard for the King's birthday.

or wounded by the military in the wake of massive protests that called for the resignation of non-elected Prime Minister, Suchinda Kraprayoon. These events jolted the country to the brink of chaos and were only resolved by the intervention of King Bhumipol, the reigning monarch, who advocated reconciliation amongst the different parties. Although a stable, democratically elected government has since taken over, the events of May 1992 serve as a reminder of the past and of the uncertain political future that still overshadows Thailand. **19**

Where to Go

Bangkok

Thailand's capital might well come as a shock to the senses, but there is plenty to see for anyone prepared to put up with the heat and confusion. From its huge shopping malls, shady temples and bustling markets, to its restaurants, sleepy canals and brazen nightlife, Bangkok offers endless surprises. King Rama I modelled the city on

Ayutthaya, with its canals that crisscross the city and magnificent temples. Much of the old town has been replaced by the bursting metropolis which extends on all sides, but there are still beautiful temples as well as palaces, historical buildings and, of course, Bangkok's notorious nightclubs.

The great distances and the heat make it one of the world's least walkable cities, and aimless sauntering may result in nothing but a twisted ankle, for the pavements are chronically torn up. Three preferable options are to find yourself a taxi, a *tuk tuk* (three-wheeled motorbike scooter) or coach tour, which can be arranged in any hotel. Ideas – in addition to a selection of leaflets – on what to do are given by the Tourism Authority of Thailand (TAT) on Bamrung Muang Road.

It is worth remembering that pleasure in Bangkok is usually

Ginger, lime and chillis add spice to even the humblest market stalls.

equal to effort – the more you put into the place, the more you'll enjoy it; and those that do take the time and trouble will discover one of the great capitals of the East.

*R*ice barges on the mighty Chao Phya River, as seen from Wat Arun on the west bank.

MAJOR DISTRICTS

Before you set out to explore the city, take a tip and buy a map. Only with an extremely detailed and up-to-date city plan will you be able to take on the unplanned chaos that is Bangkok. What's more, don't expect to find a town centre, for the city's sights are widely spread, with several major districts vying for attention. Start off your tour with the greatest monuments, and head for the area called **Royal Bangkok**, which is situated just a stone's throw from the river. This is the oldest part of the city, and is home to Wat Arun and Wat Pho, as well as the magnificent Grand Palace (see p.23).

To the south is one of Bangkok's original shopping centres. The **New Road** (which is also known as Charoen Krung Road) lies around the General Post Office and was the first official road in Thailand. This area is still well supplied with gift shops and 'instant' tailors. Several churches and embassies are situated between Charoen Krung and the river, as is the celebrated Oriental Hotel, once the haunt of such figures as Joseph Conrad, Noel Coward and Somerset Maugham.

You may not find celebrities in **Chinatown** (the lively district off Charoen Krung), but you will see a profusion of entrepreneurs. Take a walk along Soi Wanit (formerly known as Sampang Lane), with its shops selling Chinese lanterns, wigs, shark fin soup and gold necklaces. Follow it up with a visit to the busy markets at Ratchawong and Yaowarat Roads.

Cinemas and tailors, as well as more up-market shopping and eating, are offered at the **Siam Square** area. When it's hot, everyone takes refuge in the air-conditioned splendour of its five-storey shopping centres and plush boutiques. Keep an eye open for the city's most important spirit house on the corner of Rajadamri Road and Ploenchit Road. The **Erawan Shrine** was built by the owners of the former Erawan Hotel following various mishaps, the final straw being the sinking at sea of a ship bringing marble to the hotel. There have been no further incidents since the shrine was finished, and today a steady stream of the faithful arrive to offer flowers, boiled eggs and bottles of whisky to the resident spirits.

Further east, across the railway tracks leading all the way to Chiang Mai, Ploenchit Road becomes **Sukhumvit Road**. This marks the start of a rambling shopping, entertainment and residential area; be warned if you are trying to find somewhere specific, though, for all the side roads (*sois*) have numbers as opposed to names, and wherever you go it is imperative that you have the full numerical address.

A final area to contend with lies to the south, along Silom

Road. This is home to the business district and to the best-known street of all: **Patpong**, that small plot of land which started as a rice terrace and is now possibly the most famous red-light district in the world.

 ## The Grand Palace

If you have time for only one sight in Bangkok, then make it the Grand Palace, the fabulous city within a city which is situated a short stroll to the east of the river, near the Tha Chang pier. Begun in 1782 during the reign of King Rama I, and refined and enlarged by successive Chakri monarchs, this one square mile (2.5sq km) area has been transformed into an incomparable, fairytale world of jewel-encrusted monuments and spires.

Make sure you allow at least a couple of hours – enough to give you a sense of the place – and don't forget that flipflops and shorts are banned, so respectful dress is required.

A pair of 200-year-old lions – Chinese stone sculptures – stand fiercely before the gate leading to the **Audience Hall of Dusit Maha Prasad**. These flamboyant statues are said to have reached Bangkok as ballast on Chinese junks fetching Thai rice.

The current Dusit Hall was built in 1789 on the site of an earlier building that was struck by lightning. Although not the original, it has a traditional gilded, nine-tier roof supported by four *garudas* (large mythical birds), which are clasping dragon-headed serpents.

On the edge of the square, near the Hall, you will see an elegant, white-marble building known as the Disrobing Pavilion. This was where the king would alight from his carriage and adjust his ceremonial hat, before entering the throne room.

Even more impressive is the **Chakri Maha Prasad**, which is the centrepiece of the whole complex. It was built by the internationally-minded Rama V, and blends Asian and Italian Renaissance styles. Of particular note are the central balcony and approach stairway. These are topped by a traditional roof which rises in stages to three **23** seven-tiered spires. Below the central spire stands a golden urn which contains the ashes of the Chakri kings.

To the east is the **Audience Hall of Amarindra**. Built during the reign of Rama I, it contains two thrones, the upper in the shape of a boat, the lower covered by a magnificent nine-tiered, white canopy.

Among all this 'King and I' architecture, one palace in particular stands out above all the others. **Wat Phra Kaeo**, the royal chapel and Temple of the

*B*angkok's best known monument – the Grand Palace. More gold is added every year to ensure it keeps its shine.

Emerald Buddha, is covered in finery unrivalled by anything, or anywhere else in Thailand, protected by a nine-tiered umbrella, and surrounded by gold murals. The Emerald Buddha itself stands just 75cm (30in) tall and is made of jade. Thais believe that so long as it remains in their hands, Thailand will be safe. Such is the veneration for the Emerald Buddha that each season the king himself dresses the image in different robes: gilded gold and sapphires in the rainy season; a diamond robe for summer; and woven saffron in winter.

Inside the royal chapel, photography and shoes are forbidden – you'll be reminded to take off your shoes outside. As you sit on the floor, take in the grandeur of the scene, but remeber to make sure (here as in all temples) that your feet do not point towards the altar.

On the way out you can also visit the modestly named **Coin Museum**. Displayed in glass cases in two jail-like enclaves are gold coins and swords, and crown jewels, all dating from the 11th century.

Six Great Wats

Visit six of Bangkok's *wats* – monasteries or temples – as part of your tour of its greatest architectural wonders, but do make sure that you leave plenty of time, as distances can be quite considerable.

One of the best-known landmarks, the splendid **Wat Arun** (Temple of Dawn), stands on the opposite bank of the Chao Phya River in Thon Buri, but is only a minute or two away by ferry. The temple was built during the first half of the 19th century by Rama II and Rama III, and is decorated with millions of fragments of porcelain arranged in the shape of flowers. The central tower is taller than a 20-storey building and affords stunning views across the river – but the stairs are steep and the exit narrow. Photographers and anyone not so appreciative of heights are better to sit on the opposite bank of the river at sunset.

Wat Pho, Bangkok's oldest monastery, houses an incredible, 16th-century, gilt, reclining Buddha in its vast white **25**

What's a Wat?

Although you will see *wats* or Buddhist temples everywhere in Thailand, you may find it something of a problem getting to grips with their specialized vocabulary. Here's a brief rundown of the most common architectural terms:

bot: temple where religious rites are held.

chedi: bell-like dome, often containing holy relics.

chofa: graceful ornament extending from the roof.

prang: cylinder with rounded top, pointing up like a finger.

stupa: tower or pagoda, often a burial site.

viharn: preaching or worship hall.

enclosure. Almost 15m (50ft) high and 46m (150ft) long, it reaches right up to the roof of the temple. On the feet, inlaid with mother-of-pearl, are the 108 auspicious characteristics of the Buddha.

A tall teak structure painted red and called the Giant Swing stands incongruously outside the monastery of **Wat Suthat**. In former years, death-defying swingers used to show off their acrobatic skills during the annual Brahmin harvest festival. The show has not been held since 1935, however, when it was stopped after several of the faithful lost their balance. Don't miss one of Bangkok's most beautiful (and largest) Buddhas at the temple nearby. Outside, graceful, bronze horses stand at the four corners of the building.

Wat Saket, better known as the Golden Mount, can be seen long before you reach it. It sits atop Bangkok's only hill – and an artificial one at that – surmounted by a big gold *chedi*. Spiral steps up the mount's reinforced sides lead to a viewing platform. Take a map with you to identify the palaces and temples spread out below. The faithful make the climb less for the view than for the shrine containing relics of the Buddha. These were given to King Rama V in 1897 by Lord Curzon, Viceroy of India.

The best time to visit **Wat Benchamabophit**, the Marble Temple, is at dawn, when the graceful marble is still tinged with orange and the monks are queueing for their daily alms. Built at the turn of the century, it is thought to be the finest instance of recent temple architecture in the city. It is a haven of calm, with its inner courtyard surrounded by statues of the Buddha, and its ponds filled with plump fish and turtles, fed daily with papaya and bananas by the monks and other believers. Outside and past the canal are the monks' quarters, set amongst green lawns.

The impressive Buddha at **Wat Traimit** might have remained concealed forever had it not been for workmen extending the port of Bangkok, who dropped the then stucco-covered statue from a crane, revealing the vast Buddha inside. This is Thailand's largest

Bangkok's Wat Phra Kaeo temple, home to the national symbol of the Emerald Buddha.

gold image; weighing 5 tons and dating from the Sukhothai period, when it was probably disguised to keep it out of the hands of the warring Burmese. **27**

Museums and Palaces

On Na Phra That Road, a short walk from the Grand Palace, the **National Museum** houses Thailand's finest collection of antiquities. The sculpture, ceramics and jewellery here offer fine insight into the country's unique synthesis of different cultures – as well as the sheer variety of the kingdom's artefacts. Try to be there for a tour (ask at TAT offices for times), lest you be overwhelmed by the size and scope of the place.

The earliest works – from excavations at Ban Chiang in north-east Thailand – are the most interesting: pots and jars with bold designs in the shape of fingerprints – the haunting patterns are curiously modern, and yet the pottery is probably 5,000 years old.

The museum exhibition divides Thai culture into several periods, starting off with the Dvaravati (AD 6th-11th centuries), then tracing the development of political power to Lan Na, Sukhothai, Ayutthaya, and ultimately Bangkok (late 18th-century to present-day art is also known as Ratanakosin). As you go through the rooms, arranged chronologically, you can see the changes in the portrayal of the Buddha, the overriding theme of Thai art.

The museum offers a range of other things to see, from a 20-ton royal funeral chariot – which needed over 290 people to push it – to thrones, litters, 19th-century Thai typewriters, and even a full-size model elephant fitted out for battle.

A different sort of museum is situated in the magnificent edifice which is known as **Jim Thompson's house**, located to the east of the city off a smelly little canal. Bringing a sense of calm to even the most frenetic of days, the cool timber rooms of this teak house (open Monday to Friday) are packed with priceless artefacts, sculptures and ceramics.

The story of Jim Thompson is as intriguing as his taste in art. A New York architect, he came to South East Asia as a secret agent in World War II. Settling in Bangkok after the war, he converted the Thai silk industry from a primitive craft into international big business. In 1967 he vanished while on holiday in neighbouring Malaysia. The mystery is still unsolved. No trace of Thompson has ever been found, but this monument, 'the house on the *klong*' (canal), is as he left it.

The huge palace known as **Vimanmek** (Celestial Residence) might lack mystery, but it's certainly not short of scale. It was built during the reign of King Chulalongkorn, is reputed to be the largest teak building in the world, and contains an impressive collection of objets d'art, paintings and royal jewellery, plus the first shower ever installed in Thailand. Recently restored under the patronage of Queen Sirikit, the palace is now open daily.

One final building not to be missed is the **Suan Pakkard Palace** on Sri Ayutthaya Road. This superb building is owned by Princess Chumbot and surrounded by leafy gardens that are home to a gruff but friendly pelican. Down at the bottom of the impeccable garden stands the delightful Lacquer Pavilion, which is believed to be the only house of its type to survive the sack of Ayutthaya in 1767. Bought in 1959, the pavilion was then rebuilt here as a gift to the Princess from her late husband. Some of the inside walls are covered with exquisite paintings – gold leaf on black lacquer – which illustrate scenes in the life of the Buddha and episodes from the national legend, the *Ramakien*. Suan Pakkard (which literally translates as 'lettuce garden') is open daily except Sunday.

BANGKOK AFLOAT

The most popular way of exploring the fascinating *klongs* (canals) which are so central to Bangkok's character, is to take either a tour from Tha Chang pier near the Grand Palace, or a similar trip arranged by any of the hotels. A one-hour tour, (including a visit to the snake farm, see p.31) is quite expensive, but will take you to sections of old Thon Buri that you would hardly dream still existed – past floating restaurants and petrol stations, old wooden houses and temples.

29

Once there was a colourful floating market here, but these days you will have to go all the way to Damnoen Saduak (see p.34) to find the real thing.

Most river tours leave early in the morning and include a visit to the **royal barges** in their shed in Klong Bangkok Noi. All the ceremonial craft are like dreamboats come true – other-worldly vessels trimmed with fanciful prows and elaborate red and gold decorations. The king's own boat is propelled by 50 oarsmen.

You can explore the canals on your own by means of the local shuttle boats, long-tailed *hang yaos*. These long, narrow craft, powered by noisy truck engines, carry the propeller on

Thrilling scenes from early Thai history are depicted in this mural at the Grand Palace.

30

the end of a long drive shaft –
hence their name, 'long-tailed'
boats. You can also hire your
own *hang yao* by the hour –
but as with taxis, be sure to
agree on a price in advance.

Down Klong Bangkok Noi
(Small Canal) and Klong Yai
(Big Canal), handsome houses
with gardens and fountains are
squashed cheek by jowl with
old, wooden houses on stilts,
shaded by palm trees. Nearby
you will see rubber tyre factories and temples, floating supermarkets and snack bars. The
canals are filled with children
and shy, young women scrub-
bing clothes or daintily brush-
ing their teeth in the gruesome
coloured water.

Anyone who prefers slower
and cheaper transport can take
one of the public water taxis
known as Chao Phya Express
Boats that travel up and down
the river at regular 20-minute
intervals. If you start either at
the landing alongside the Oriental Hotel, or Tha Chang pier
near the Grand Palace, you can
spend 90 minutes passing by
some of Bangkok's greatest
monuments, although you will

have to get off at Nonthaburi,
which is the end of the line. Be
warned, though: getting a seat
is not always that easy, and a
lengthy stand in the heat can
be a painful experience.

Once at Nonthaburi, a small
market is the main point of interest. The last boats return at
6pm, after which you can only
take a more expensive taxi.

DIVERSIONS

Bored of temples? Fed up with
museums and canals? Then try
one of the following:

Chatuchak Market. Don't
forget to bring your camera to
Chatuchak, for this is the most
extensive and mind-numbing
collection of stalls that you can
imagine. Anything from wigs
to pot plants and herbal cures
for insomnia is available. Take
note, though, Chatuchak opens
on Saturday and Sunday only,
from dawn to dusk.

Snake farm. At the Pasteur
Institute, where Henri Durant
and Rama IV roads meet, ven-
omous, striped, banded kraits
are the pick of the bunch. All
the wriggling specimens here **31**

are owned by Thailand's Red Cross, which supplies medical centres throughout the kingdom with snake bite serum. Cobras with hypnotic patterns, spotted vipers and other just as deadly snakes are milked for humanity – and visitor interest – every morning at 11 o'clock.

Dusit Zoo. The Thais themselves don't come to Dusit Zoo to see the wildlife in its natural habitat, but to watch elephants and deer beg food. In the off-colour pond, where romantic couples go boating, giant turtles even try to consume Coca-Cola bottles. Apart from the animals and admirably landscaped aviary, the zoo is probably the best place in Bangkok just to watch the Thai people having fun. Open every day.

Lumpini Park. Lumpini is a relative haven of peace in the city centre. Thais come here at the weekend to picnic and indulge in the art of *sanuk* (good time). In addition to stalls selling kebabs and noodles, at the park's northern exit (leading to Soi Sarasin), there is a bar and restaurant from where you can watch the sun go down.

Around Bangkok

The following excursions are all easily reached from Bangkok, and make rewarding side-trips or useful stepping stones on the way north or south.

WEST OF BANGKOK

Rose Garden and Nakhon Pathom

One hour's drive to the west of Bangkok's heat and tumult lies the cool and calm Rose Garden. The roses constitute only a small part of 20ha (50 acres) of blissful tropical gardens. A cultural performance is staged daily at 3pm featuring folk and classical dances, sword fights, Thai boxing and a traditional Thai wedding. In addition you can take a ride on an elephant or even be photographed wrapped up in a monstrously long, but guaranteed 'tame' python.

From the Rose Garden, continue 30km (20 miles) west to the town of Nakhon Pathom (believed to be Thailand's oldest), home to the biggest *chedi* in the country. King Mongkut built the pagoda, which resembles an upside-down ice-cream cone, in the middle of the 19th century on top of the ruins of an ancient temple dating back over 1,000 years. During the 1970s, this new *chedi* almost collapsed, but prompt action by the Fine Arts Department saved the day and it can still be seen in all its glory.

Also at Nakhon Pathom is the **Sanam Chan Palace**. This modern structure is entirely in traditional Thai style, with the exception of an English Tudor building, which was once used as a setting for Shakespeare plays. Note, also, the statue of the dog named Yalay, who was greatly mourned by Rama VI after allegedly being poisoned by jealous courtiers.

Floating Market

You won't need a guide to take you to the floating market at **Damnoen Saduak** – everyone is running tours there nowadays. Nonetheless, the diminutive boats piled with coconuts, bananas and durian remain as authentic as ever – almost.

Try to get there early, while the women in broad-brimmed hats are out in full force, paddling along the narrow canals and haggling for a bunch of chillies or barbecued fish. Photographers might want to walk along the edge of the canal, or stop on the wooden bridges, which make excellent spots for observing. For a few hundred baht, a boat can even be arranged to paddle you out into the centre of the fray.

At another tourist market on shore, you can buy Burmese carpets, wooden carvings and other such things. Unfortunately, however, the goods are, on the whole, expensive, and you would be better to buy them in Bangkok or Chiang Mai.

Some excursions might include a visit to a nearby snake sideshow, where handlers in bare feet are keen to show their courage and expertise.

Kanchanaburi

Kanchanaburi's calm, lush setting on the banks of the **Kwai River** belies its history, for it was here during World War II that thousands of prisoners-of-war died building the famous 'Bridge over the River Kwai', as recounted in Pierre Boulle's novel and the film based on it.

You can still see the bridge, minus a couple of original sections, which were bombed in 1945, and two trains cross it every day on their way to the town of Nam Toc (waterfall), a

Floating markets like Damnoen Saduak have almost become a thing of the past.

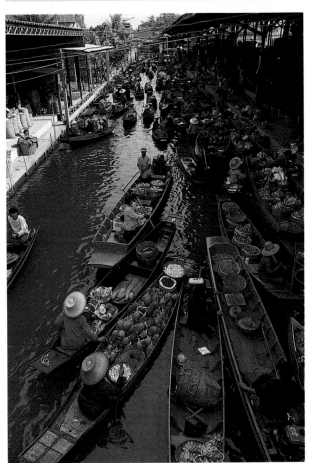

pleasant hour's journey further to the west.

To get an idea of the horrors of building the bridge, visit the two cemeteries which contain over 8,000 graves of British, Dutch, Australian, Malaysian, Indian, New Zealand, Canadian and Burmese prisoners and conscripts who, together with almost 60,000 civilians, died during the railway's construction. The inscriptions on the gravestones are as simple and moving as tragic poems.

Those prepared to risk being run over by motorscooters and jostled by the crowds of locals should walk over the bridge to the other side. A safer way to view this tragic monument is from the long-tailed boats that hurtle up and down the river, stopping off at the cemetery and nearby caves.

Afterwards, you can drop in at the **Jeath Museum** on the river bank. Housed in a type of bamboo hut discovered in the prison camps, the exhibition documents Japanese atrocities in photographs, paintings and relics. It also reveals the prisoners' ingenuity in surviving

great hardships, as well as the sympathy and help which was secretly offered to the inmates by the local Thai population.

If you want to explore the countryside, adventurous businessmen have set up bases for tourists north west of Kanchanaburi, in some of the most unspoilt scenery in the country. One hotel, next to the river, pampers its guests with air-conditioning and a swimming pool, while a couple of others, slightly more spartan, are built on bamboo rafts floating in the stream. Excursions to waterfalls, caves and national parks can be arranged from these advance camps.

NORTH OF BANGKOK

Ayutthaya

Undoubtedly the most enjoyable way to get to the ancient capital of Ayutthaya is by taking the luxurious cruiser down the Chao Phya River that departs every day from outside the Oriental Hotel. On the way you will go past factories and warehouses and, further afield, rice fields and the beginnings of the countryside that stretches to Nakhon Sawan and the source of the Chao Phya River hundreds of miles away.

Before exploring the great archaeological site itself, most tours call in at the nearby royal estate of **Bang Pa-in**. This fine little palace was built by King Prasat Thong in the 17th century, and subsequently used as a summer residence by future kings. The names of buildings like 'the Excellent and Shining Abode' and 'the Sage's Lookout' are as delightful as the structures themselves. However, nothing beats the splendid **Aisawan Tippaya Asna** (The Divine Seat of Personal Freedom), situated in the middle of the lake by which King Chulalongkorn (Rama V) composed odes as the sun went down.

Back on the highway, continue 20km (12 miles) south to the town of Ayutthaya, former capital of Thailand and home to one of its greatest civilizations. Here, where cattle still graze, you can climb the steps of ruined temples to look over

the immensity of the ruined city, which was laid waste by the Burmese, who sacked the capital in 1767. In the shade of a solitary wall, let your imagination re-create the opulence of that bygone era.

*W*ith 375 temples and 29 fortresses to see, Ayutthaya is best explored with a cyclo-driver. **37**

Founding a Dynasty

According to legend, Ayutthaya was founded by the illegitimate son of a princess, who was discovered to be pregnant after eating an aubergine on which a gardener had relieved himself! U-Thong, or Prince of the Golden Crib, as the son was named, became the first of 33 ruling kings, while the kingdom became the largest and most beautiful in the Orient and the principal one in Siam for over four centuries.

There are dozens of distinctive buildings, and you will be hard pressed to visit Ayutthaya in one day. For a tour of the ruins, it's best to start at **Wat Phra Si Sanphet**, on Si Sanphet Road, near the tourist car park. The temple was built in 1448 and once housed a 16m (50ft) Buddha image covered in gold and weighing 170kg (375lb). In 1767 the Burmese set fire to it in order to melt off the gold, destroying both temple and image. What you can see are restored *chedis*, which hold the ashes of King Borom Trai Lokanat and his two sons.

At **Wat Phra Ram**, a graceful 14th-century building that is positioned amidst reflecting pools, there is a beautiful cloister lined with stone Buddha images, as well as several elephant gates, mythical *nagas* and *garudas*. The temple was built in 1369 by King Ramesuan, on the site where his father was cremated.

For an overview of the art of the age of Ayutthaya, visit the **Chao Sam Phraya Museum**, stocked with the best statues discovered in the ruins. There are beautiful bronze Buddhas dating from the 13th and 14th centuries, as well as 17th- and 18th-century door panels with religious, traditional or flower carvings, and a great hoard of 15th-century gold jewellery.

Next, visit **Wat Mahathat**, built in 1384 by King Ramesuan. Once, it contained treasures of precious stones, gold and crystal, and a relic of the Lord Buddha in a gold casket, which is now housed in the National Museum (see p.28).

38

Wat Rachaburan, next to Wat Mahathat, was built in the 15th century around the tombs of Prince Ay and Prince Yi, brothers who slew each other in a tragic battle on elephant-back. Rare frescoes remain in the crypt, but any portable antiquities were stolen years ago.

Finish off with a visit to the **Elephant Kraal**, a few miles from town, where hunters used to drive large herds (up to 200 animals) of wild elephants into the stockade. Once captured they were put into the king's service, either as fighters or, if they were the rare white type, as symbols of power. The last capture was in 1903 during the reign of King Chulalongkorn.

SOUTH EAST OF BANGKOK

Ancient City

If your time is limited, there is no need to go to Sukhothai and Ayutthaya to see the ancient capitals. A far-sighted temple buff made the trip unnecessary by building models of them in what is said to be the largest outdoor museum in the world, 33km (20 miles) south east of Bangkok. Laid out as a map of Thailand and covering roughly 81ha (200 acres), Ancient City re-creates the country's greatest buildings in either full-size or slightly reduced scale. The parks also boast exotic birds,

Thailand's most beloved animal is as popular as ever, but sadly, numbers are dwindling.

39

monkeys and elephants, which keep the children happy. Travel agents run half-day outings to Ancient City, or there are daily buses from Bangkok.

Crocodile Farm

Another 5km (3 miles) along the road from Ancient City is the Crocodile Farm at Samut Prakarn. This huge enclosure is billed as the world's largest establishment of its kind, with the total 'croc' population put at almost 50,000. The farm has two purposes: it preserves endangered species, at the same time as entertaining and educating the public as a zoo.

You will see literally thousands of crocodiles of all ages, shapes and sizes here, most of them basking self-indulgently in the sun. Not all last long, with many ending up as handbags, belts or wallets, or even stuffed for display purposes. A few of the big fellows have a more theatrical role, wrestling with a handler for the tourists. The travel agencies in Bangkok run half-day tours, or you can take a bus there yourself.

NORTH EAST OF BANGKOK

Khao Yai

The vast national park at Khao Yai rises from the Korat plateau, baked dry in summer and lush with greenery and flowers following the rains. Khao Yai means 'big mountain', and the resort, which is located three-hours' drive from Bangkok, is both the oldest and one of the best in the kingdom.

Tired of waiting for dinner ... or just eaten? It's a crocodile's life at Samut Prakarn.

The park covers 2,100sq km (837 sq miles), and within its boundaries are elephants and over 100 other species, including Asian wild dog, clouded leopard and black bear, all still running wild. Keep an eye out for some of Thailand's most significant bird concentrations, among which are some of the largest groups of hornbills in South East Asia, moustached barbets, orange-breasted and red-headed trogons, and great slaty woodpeckers.

Although wildlife sightings are neither consistently common nor, for that matter, guaranteed, pleasant walks to giant waterfalls help to occupy any spare time, and night-time safaris are organized with spotlights to pick out deer, tropical birds and, if you're lucky, tigers and bears.

Before being declared a national park in 1959, Khao Yai was known as a sanctuary not just for animals, but also as a popular hiding place for outlaws. This, of course, is no longer the case, and now the park offers hotels, a restaurant, and an 18-hole golf course.

Nakhon Ratchasima (Korat) and Phimai

A statue of the city's heroine, Khunying Mo, is often the first thing that visitors notice at the agreeable but unexciting town of Korat – officially known as Nakhon Ratchasima. It's likely that you won't stay here long, except to look at the modern, controversial Buddhist temple of **Wat Sala Loi**, which calls to mind contemporary Western church architecture. Inside is a massive white Buddha, as big as a house.

If time is short, it's better to head straight to Phimai, some 68km (42 miles) north east, for its ancient religious compound at the end of the long, dusty main street.

Built during King Jayavarman VI's reign in the 12th century, and situated just a short distance from the Cambodian border, Phimai was probably designed by Khmer architects, for it is similar in style to the magnificent Angkor Wat (see p.94). Four gates dominate the ruins, the largest preceded by a *naga* bridge guarded by lions. **41**

Adorning the elegant arcades of the cloisters are intricate engravings of flowers, elephants and monkeys.

Inside the inner courtyard stand two small *stupas* (Prang Hin Daeng and Prang Phromathat), and in the centre there is an ornate dome with doors and a lintel, intricately carved with Mahayana Buddhism scenes.

Outside in the gardens there is an open-air museum, which contains a collection of ancient friezes, statues, and stone lintels of Buddha, gods and monkeys. These were gathered all over north-east Thailand prior to being amassed here.

A pleasant way to round off the trip is to visit the larger-than-life (or at least taller than a house) **banyan tree**, which stands 2km (1.2 miles) further down the road and is said to be the biggest in the world. Delicious Isaan food is served in its shade, but only in the dry season. During the wet season, the nearby reservoir floods the picnic ground. If spirits live in trees – as many Thais believe – then this prodigious banyan is surely thronged with ghosts.

Pattaya

Visitors rarely come to Pattaya for palm-fringed beaches and tropical seas, for this infamous resort, sited 147km (91 miles) south east of Bangkok, lost its original attractions to pollution many years ago. What Pattaya does have – and in abundance – is fun, along with a nightlife that eclipses even Bangkok.

Although King Taksin once set up camp in the vicinity 200 years ago, he failed to give the seashore a second thought. In the ensuing years, little of consequence happened to the village until 1961, when the first American servicemen arrived for what was soon described as 'R & R' – rest and recreation. The Thais eventually realized Pattaya's commercial possibilities, and the area fast became a thriving international resort.

Today, there are over 20,000 hotel rooms or bungalows here officially considered to meet with international standards of comfort. Hundreds more, suitable for budget travellers, are found near the seafront strip, surrounded by bars and clubs.

Most hotels have swimming pools, since these days the sea around Pattaya is not recommended. Indeed, if swimming is what you are after, take a boat trip to the outlying coral islands. Alternatively, catch a *baht* bus to the beach at Jomtien, a 15-minute trip south, where clean sand stretches for several miles, with only a few glistening new condominiums.

Adventurous visitors to Pattaya might consider trying out parasailing, while others may prefer a day's deep-sea fishing, relishing the opportunity to try catching delicious snapper and sizeable marlin. Countless excursion boats take tourists to islands in the surrounding area for swimming and snorkelling in clear blue seas.

At **Ko Larn**, about 45 minutes from Pattaya in a converted trawler, or half the time in a speedboat, you can explore the underwater world in a glass-bottomed boat, gazing at vivid tropical fish and coral – albeit now sadly depleted compared with a few years ago. Some scuba expeditions begin here with a workout, before going on to a couple of wrecks which lie further south, near Sattahip.

Land tours are just as easy to arrange, and you might visit **Nong Nooch**, an exotic village 15km (9 miles) to the east, for daily displays of folk dances, martial arts and (the controversial) cock fighting, as well as a vast acreage of exotic palms, orchids and cacti. If that's not your scene, try **Mini Siam**, a miniature town which contains more than 100 historic towns on a scale of 1:25, or there is always the **Elephant Kraal**, where elephants show off their strength, skill and obedience. Keen equestrians should head for **Reo Park Ranch**, 30 minutes from Pattaya, for a gallop on thoroughbreds.

When you return, there are plenty of culinary delights as well, since the restaurants in Pattaya serve first-rate seafood – shrimp, clams, crab, lobster, oyster, prawns and a variety of others. What's more, you don't have to be in luxury hotels to feast on such delights; simple, waterfront restaurants provide dishes that are just as tasty, but at a fraction of the 5-star price. **43**

Those who prefer French fries and *bratwurst* shouldn't worry either – you'll be just as well catered for as everyone else.

Pattaya's nightlife, too, has something to satisfy almost all tastes, from big musical productions and the world-famous transvestite shows, to discos, nightclubs, beer bars – and all those other establishments that have earned this area its reputation of the international entertainment resort of Thailand.

Hua Hin

You can easily bypass Pattaya and opt for quieter charms at Hua Hin, 220km (137 miles) south of Bangkok, which has long been a favourite beach resort of the royal family, as well as most other Thais. The odd condominium has blotted out some of its royal views, and its long, sweeping beaches are no longer as pleasant as they once were for swimming, although they do still make fine strolling ground. However, with its lazy beaches, deckchairs, pony riding and golf courses, Hua Hin is far removed from Pattaya.

Central Thailand

The most striking thing about the central region is its sheer abundance; for this vast, fertile plain that starts at Bangkok's busy outskirts is the country's rice bowl, home to one third of the population, and site of one of the biggest rice crops in the world. Centuries ago, this agricultural heartland also played host to some of the kingdom's greatest civilizations, amongst them those of Si Satchanalai, Sukhothai and Lop Buri, ancient cities that remain as enchanting in ruins as they must have been in their heyday.

Major towns in the area are easily visited from Bangkok, and make good stop-off points en route to the northern region.

LOP BURI

Lop Buri's dominant features are the superb stone temples

*T*he pride of Korat is the 12th-century temple at Phimai, built on the arid plains of Isaan.

built by the Khmers. These can be seen even from the railway station, as can the French-style architecture and several hundred monkeys which have become this town's other lasting claim to fame.

Originally one of the capitals of the Khmer people, Lop Buri flourished under Thai rule in the 17th century. King Narai chose the town as an alternative capital, in case some unforeseen fate befell Ayutthaya. His caution did not go without justification, as Ayutthaya was sacked by the Burmese the following century.

Begin your tour at the **Phra Narai Rajanivet Palace**. This magnificent building was constructed with the aid of French architects in the mid-17th century, and took longer than 12 years to complete. Inside is the National Museum, housing exquisite examples of Khmer art. The palace also incorporates the old treasure houses, a banquet hall, an audience hall for high-ranking foreign visitors, and the stables where the king kept his elephants and horses.

After the palace, pay a visit to **Vichayen House**, originally the residence of the Chevalier de Chaumont, the first French ambassador to Thailand. Later it was the residence of Constantine Phaulkon (see p.13).

Harvesting the Rice

In Thailand's endless green paddies, peasant women in lampshade hats are as common a sight as water buffalo. For much of the year, up to 70 percent of the population works the fields, tilling the soil or sowing the rice, toiling from dawn to nightfall, then taking the water buffalo home, cooking and sleeping.

This is an endless cycle, dictated by the rains and the sun; those involved go on oblivious to events in the outside world. When the harvest is over, planting begins anew in time for the next rains; so it has been for centuries and so it will remain.

Near Vichayen House, **Wat Phra Si Ratana Mahathat** is a fine example of 12th-century Khmer-style architecture, with *chedis* built in Sukhothai style.

Lop Buri's famous monkeys can be found by the railway in the Kala Shrine, and in nearby Phraprang Sam Yod, a magnificent 13th-century temple with three distinctive *prangs* from which they like to hang, begging food and fruit from visitors. Make sure you keep firm hold of your camera and other valuables, as monkeys clutching stolen goods are far from an uncommon sight.

SUKHOTHAI

Sukhothai, the most striking of Thailand's various spectacular ruined cities, lies 427km (265 miles) north of Bangkok, surrounded by rice fields and distant hills. Built in the late 13th and early 14th centuries under the legendary King Ramkamhaeng, it flourished for almost 150 years until vanquished by

Life in the land of plenty – central Thailand is blessed with fine weather and rich land.

Ayutthaya, and the people fled. Until around 40 years ago, the ancient capital was hidden by jungle, the outlines of the classical towers camouflaged by a heavy green undergrowth. The situation now is better, for in a huge renovation programme implemented by Unesco and Thailand's government, some 200 moats, kilns, images and temples have been restored to the glory of earlier days. These lie within the boundaries of the historical park, 13km (8 miles) west of the new town of Sukhothai, and are reached easily by **songthaew**, reconditioned jeeps with seats in the back, which carry as many passengers as can be squeezed in.

For a delightful insight into the past and a glimpse of some of the finest sculptures, start at the **National Museum**, near to the Kamphang Hek Gate. This houses a splendid 14th-century example of the Walking Buddha, the image that, according to archaeologists, is the finest of all Thai Buddhas. A replica of King Ramkamhaeng's famous inscription is also on show. This is the earliest example of

Thai script and an oft-repeated quotation from Thai literature: 'In the water there are fish, in the fields there is rice... Those who choose to laugh, laugh, those who choose to cry, cry.'

A short walk past the moat brings you to **Wat Mahathat**, temple of the Great Relic. This is the biggest and finest temple in Sukhothai, dating from the 14th century and housing rows of the standing Buddha images known as Phra Attharot. When King Ramkamhaeng was in power, it is said that citizens would ring a bell hung outside the nearby palace to get the attention of the good monarch, who would then emerge to settle disputes and extend justice.

Continue by visiting beautiful **Wat Sra Si** (Temple of the Splendid Pond), with its graceful image of the walking Buddha and slender *chedi* shaped like a bell, and **Wat Trapang Ngoen**, situated around a large lake which floods occasionally during the rainy season.

Carry on to the west outside the walled city and you reach **Wat Sri Chum**, with its massive seated Buddha measuring

11.3m (37ft) from knee to knee, and each finger the size of a man. The sanctuary walls are 3m (10ft) thick and contain a secret passage off to the left just inside the entrance. This was used by the king, though for what purpose is not clear.

The temple of **Wat Saphan Hin** lies 2km (1.2 miles) west of the city, and is known as the Temple of the Stone Bridge, after the slate pathway leading up the hill. It is a long haul to the summit, on which stands a Buddha statue more than 12m (40ft) tall. However – and especially in the cool of the late afternoon – it is a trip that is well worth the effort.

The best time of year to visit Sukhothai is on the full moon of the 12th lunar month (mid-November), when Thailand's most beautiful and serene festival, known as *Loi Krathong*,

The ruins at Sukhothai: legend says the city was founded by a freedom fighter in 1238.

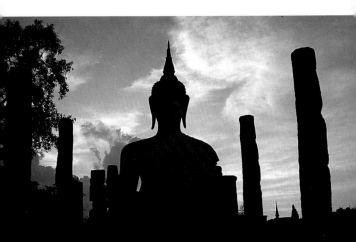

is celebrated. It is believed to have started originally some 700 years ago, after one of the king's concubines fashioned a lantern from carved fruit and sent it floating down the river bearing a lighted candle. Now, thousands of people gather by the lake to launch boats made of banana leaves and to marvel at colourful processions of the local women and a tremendous display of fireworks.

SI SATCHANALAI

If you still have a craving for more temples, you may like to consider taking an afternoon's excursion to the city of Satchanalai, 55km (35 miles) to the north of Sukhothai.

This is the sister city of Sukhothai, but is wilder and less visited by tourists, with ramshackle temples and an atmospheric air of faded grandeur. At the top of a steep flight of steps is the ruined **Wat Khao Suwankhiri**, which is worth the climb for the views alone.

Hire a bicycle from outside the historical park and explore what many regard as the city's most impressive temple, **Wat Chang Lom** (which translates literally as Elephant Temple). The *chedi* is surrounded by 39 standing elephants and a stairway which represents a ladder to heaven. Real elephants can usually be found in front of the temple, and it is often possible to get rides around the park – although they are not cheap.

In nearby Ban Khao Noi, a village 4km (2.5 miles) to the north, archaeologists have discovered kilns that might prove that the Thais began producing pottery 400 years earlier than the Chinese.

PHITSANULOK

A wide river cuts right through the heart of Phitsanulok, about 370km (230 miles) to the north of Bangkok, and separates the old part of town into two. Although the broad banks of the River Nan can make a pleasant spot to rest, the real attraction is **Wat Mahathat**.

Believers have been coming here for centuries, praying in front of the renowned golden Chinnarat Buddha, famous for its curative powers. King Ekatosarot is said to have donated gold leaf for the Buddha. The temple, with lovely mother-of-pearl doors from King Boromkot, was built in 1357, and its shrine is so popular that Thai tourists swarm here every day. To meet this demand, a variety of shops in the complex stock pendants, relics and other souvenirs by which to recall the venerated 14th-century statue.

Apart from Wat Mahathat, there are few reminders of the town's great history. A giant fire destroyed most of the old town several years ago, and now it is best known for comfortable hotels and as a base for Sukhothai excursions.

Northern Thailand

Stretching up to the Myanmar (Burma) and Laos borders and following the line of the great Mekong River, northern Thailand incorporates some of the most beautiful scenery in the country. This region was once divided into small principalities which were isolated by the rugged terrain and accessible only by elephant. Even today people speak their own dialect – influenced by Burmese and Lhao – and retain their own culinary specialities. Getting there for today's visitor, however, is a simpler process than before, with regular planes and

*F*inely-tuned poses: each statue of Buddha says something different, if you know what to look for.

51

trains leaving from Bangkok. In five days, it is easily possible to explore the area around Chiang Mai and Chiang Rai – and even to take a trek with the northern hill tribes.

CHIANG MAI

Chiang Mai, the capital of the north, rises from the banks of the Ping River, bedecked with flowers and orchid blossoms in the spring. Formerly no more than a hillside 'shangri-la', the town has grown rapidly to become both a tourist mecca and a major city in its own right – with the traffic and pollution to match. Several thousand luxury rooms and cheap and cheerful guest houses are available, as well as European-style bars and restaurants. Tour operators offer countless trips to colourful handicraft villages, hillside temples and mountain tribes.

After the heat of Bangkok, the more temperate climate of Chiang Mai comes as a relief. The cooler weather is immediately evident (pack a sweater if you're there between October and January), and so too is the abundance of fruit, vegetables and flowers, which can be seen at almost any time of year.

Chiang Mai, meaning 'new town', was founded by King Mengrai the Great at the end of the 13th century (see p.11). According to one legend, the city wall – parts of which can still be seen – was built by 90,000 men, working in shifts round-the-clock. Mengrai also built various temples and fine buildings, some of which remain and can be explored on foot or by hiring a bicycle or motorbike. Don't forget to go to the handicraft centres nearby for silk, painted umbrellas and lacquerware.

Thai Airways International flies to Chiang Mai in less than an hour from Bangkok, while air-conditioned express buses make the run in about 9 hours, and overnight express trains in 12-14 hours.

Inside the City

Start your tour of this delightful city at **Wat Chiang Man**, within the old city walls. Built in the 13th century under King

Mengrai, it contains two well-known religious statues – the Crystal and Marble buddhas, protected behind a railing, bars and glass – which were ancient long before this monastery had been conceived. Sculpted elephants surround a *chedi* at the rear of this temple.

Walk south for 15 minutes and you reach the huge, ruined *chedi* of **Wat Chedi Luang**. Built by King Saen Muang Ma in the 15th century, it was subsequently damaged during an earthquake over 400 years ago. In the temple grounds stands a gigantic gum tree shrouded in

Wherever you are in the country, Thais are expert at infusing their whole lives – appearance included – with the greatest beauty.

Orchid Mania

Some of Thailand's remote areas are happy breeding grounds for over 1,000 different varieties of orchid, ranging from the famous *Paphiopedium ascocenda* to the elegant 'Miss Udorn Sunshine'. The best place to see them is at the orchid farms in the area around Chiang Mai, although you only need to look in markets throughout the country to see and appreciate the kingdom's favourite flower.

silk which, it is said, will continue to grow for as long as the city prospers. Beneath the tree, locals leave wooden elephants and phallics as offerings to the guardian spirit of the city.

Continue west to find **Wat Phra Singh**, which contains a magnificent Buddha. According to legend, the image was on its way to the king when the chariot carrying it broke down in front of the temple. Believing this to be a signal that the image wished to go no further, the people installed it without question, and there it has remained ever since, along with a beautiful library and several fine carvings and sculptures.

The best time of day to visit **Wat Suan Dork** (The Flower Garden Temple), which is off Cherng Doy Road on the city outskirts, is at sunset when the *chedi* is bathed in soft, golden rays. The ashes of the kings of Lan Na are housed within the

Over 100 different varieties of orchid are bred at farms within reach of Chiang Mai.

temple, which is said to hold an important relic of the Buddha, brought here by elephant.

A final temple not to miss is **Wat Chedi Yot**, known as the Seven Peaks, due to its seven *chedis*. Local guides say it was inspired by a great Mahabodi Indian temple in 1455, during the reign of King Tilokaraja.

For visitors who want other entertainment, Chiang Mai has plenty to offer. Drop in at the **Banyen Folk Art Museum**, in a charming, old northern-style house, which sells some of the finest northern woodcarvings and antiques; or explore markets like **Somphet** (Moonmuang Road), or busy **Warorot** (Wichyanon Road), where you can try delicious local delicacies, including *khao soi* (a spicy noodle dish) and spicy *naem* sausages. Finally, in the evening, don't miss the **Night Market** on Changklan Road, which offers a dazzling choice of northern handicrafts. You'll be overwhelmed by the sheer variety of goods for sale – it's probably greater here than at any other market in Thailand. If all that shopping gives you

an appetite, there are plenty of restaurants to try nearby.

Outside the City

Explore the following as part of either a half-day tour or a more extended itinerary.

Elephant lovers will want to make it to the **elephant camp** at Mae Taem, 63km (39 miles) north from Chiang Mai, where you can still see the vast creatures learning the arts of timber lifting and bathing. Years ago, elephants were a common sight throughout the north, for they were used both for transport across inhospitable terrain and for dragging logs down to the river, where they could be floated downstream.

These days, elephants are the objects of more theatrical attention, with morning shows and river washing staged for visitors. You can actually have a ride on one of the giants of the jungle, and then afterwards take a raft trip through the lush countryside, alive with colourful birds.

Wooden statues, huge clay pots, and gaily coloured paper **55** umbrellas bedeck the road to the village of **Sankamphaeng**, which lies 13km (8 miles) east of Chiang Mai and is known as the handicrafts centre of north Thailand. In the factories and warehouses, you can watch the locals as they weave silk from cocoons or make lacquerware or painted umbrellas, a process that has changed little over the years. Afterwards, stock up on the best and brightest gifts in the kingdom. Purchases can be shipped home, and credit cards are widely accepted.

To visit Chiang Mai's most famous temple – and for stunning views of the surrounding region – travel the 25-minute bus ride to **Wat Phrathat Doi Suthep**, which overlooks town from atop a hill. From the car park, it's a 300-step hike (or a comfortable funicular ride) to the central gold *chedi* at the top, with its royal bronze parasols at each corner. The cloister is lined with many Buddha statues of artistic importance.

Continue another 4km (2.5 miles) past the temple to reach the **Winter Palace** (Phu-ping Palace), where the Thai king and queen often spend some of the winter. If the royal family are not in residence, at weekends and holidays the grounds are opened to the public in a blaze of lavish floral displays.

One final attraction in the vicinity is the small Hmong or Meo village called **Doi Pui**. Since it is the most accessible of all Thailand's hill tribe villages, you are unlikely to find much authenticity. Still, if you don't have enough time to go trekking, the village does give an idea of the hill tribes' way of life, and also includes a visit to the opium museum. Crowds of children sell colourful costumes, tassled bags and primitive handicrafts.

TREKKING

To see the tribes in a more authentic environment, go along with an organized trek into the hills. You will probably have to walk considerable distances and sleep on less than luxurious floors, but with a guide's aid, you can still locate numerous Karen tribes, who believe in the spirits of the winds and the rains, or the Lahu people, the men in silver buckles and black turbans and women in calf-length tunics with yellow or white embroidery.

Known as the *chao doi*, the hill tribes are nomadic peoples who have migrated from Tibet and southern China along various routes into Burma, Thailand and Laos. In all, there are some 500,000 of them, divided into six tribes: the Karen, Meo, Akha, Yao, Lisu and Lahu, all

A bunch of artificial flowers still catches the eye of passers-by in Chiang Mai's market.

with their own distinct dress, language and culture.

Generally, they are highland dwellers who opt to live above 1,000m (3,280ft). They earn a living from foraging, slash and burn agriculture and domestic **57** livestock such as chickens and black pigs; all inter-tribe trade is done by barter. Traditionally the *chao doi* have also shared a common mythology. They believe that they live on top of a dragon and that they have to keep the peace to ensure that it does not move.

The Karen: of all the tribes, the Karen or Yang Karing are the most numerous, their population standing at approximately 265,000. Concentrated on the whole in the mountainous area along the western border with Burma, they are probably the oldest tribe, having been in Thailand for over 250 years.

The Meo: the next largest group is the Meo (Hmong), who are found mainly around Chiang Mai, Chiang Rai and Mae Hong Son. One of the proudest of the tribal people, they worship the spirit of the sky, which they believe created the world and their way of life.

The Akha: thought to number roughly 33,000, the Akha came from Yunnan in southern China and live mainly in extended family units, which are a hallmark of traditional Akha life. Worshipping the sun and moon, the Akhas also fear the spirits in the swamps and termite mounds, and offer chickens to appease them.

The Yao: the Yao are found mainly in the surroundings of Chiang Rai, Phayao and Nan, and can often be identified by their teeth capped with gold – a popular sign of wealth – their ankle-length tunics, and thick, purple sashes around the neck. The Yao have traditionally cultivated opium and believe in polygamous marriages and extended families.

The Lisu: spread throughout nine northern provinces, the most widely dispersed hill tribe is the Lisu. In total there are around 24,000 of them, divided into the black Lisu and Hua Lisu. They only started to migrate roughly 60 years ago, coming from southern China.

The Lahu: of Tibetan origin, the Lahu are poorer than other tribes and number somewhere in the region of 55,000. They are mainly concentrated north of Chiang Rai and in the Fang area, and you can often distinguish the men by their silver buckles and black turbans, and the women by calf-length tunics with embroidery.

Travel agencies in Chiang Mai operate excursions ranging from one-day trips to more rewarding three- and four-day expeditions. Don't expect too much originality, though – villagers may ask for payment for posing for photos, and while some are friendly and seem to be pleased that their colourful bejewelled costumes and simple huts are a centre of attention, others have discarded just about every trace of their traditions, opting instead for jeans, T-shirts and Pepsi Cola.

It's always worth dropping in to the tourist office to check which are the reliable trekking

Treks to tribal villages make fascinating visits as well as earning revenue for the local people.

companies, as they can change from month to month. Be sure to use a guide who can speak English and, if at all possible, the tribal tongue as well, since this will greatly add to the success of the trip.

LAMPHUN

Although legend has it that the most beautiful women in Thailand are from Lamphun, this is not the only reason for coming to this peaceful, ancient town, which can be found 30km (18 miles) south of Chiang Mai.

A large, historical monastery in the town centre called **Wat Phrathat Haripunchai** is a busy educational and meditational institution. The huge, gold *chedi* in the middle of the monastery was begun over one thousand years ago, and the workmen who erected it constructed their own simpler version outside the compound; it is now a ruin with trees sprouting from it. Close by and built in modern style is the National Museum, which has a collection of sculptures found in the Lamphun district, dating from the 10th to 12th centuries. One unusual exhibit is a slender-barrelled Chinese cannon from the Ming dynasty.

You can take a pedicab from the centre of Lamphun to **Wat Chama Devi** (or Ku Kut), a temple that owes its existence to Princess Chama Devi, who is said to have founded it when she ruled the Mon kingdom of Lamphun well over a thousand years ago. Of the original elements, the most memorable is a *chedi* rising in five tiers with 60 standing Buddha images of stucco around the sides.

Look out for the *lamyai* orchards that have helped make this region famous throughout Thailand. This fruit, known as longan in English, resembles a lychee and is delicious.

LAMPANG

Don't be surprised if you see a horse and carriage slowly trundling down the main road of this beautiful old town, 100km (62 miles) south east of Chiang Mai – this is Lampang's main form of transport, and the best way to explore.

There are three temples that deserve special mention. **Wat Phra Fang** boasts a tall, white *chedi* with seven small shrines around the base. **Wat Phra Kaew Do Toa Suchadaram** reveals Burmese influence and has outstanding carvings. **Wat Phrathat Lampang Luang**, situated 18km (11 miles) from Lampang near the town of Ko Kha, is worth a visit for its museum and fine Buddha images.

Lampang's history is as fascinating as its temples. Once the capital of the ancient Mon kingdom, before the Thai people arrived, in the 16th century the town attained a mystic sort of renown because of a stubborn elephant. The story tells us that the much revered statue known as the Emerald Buddha was being transported to Chiang Mai when the elephant refused to go beyond Lampang. This was taken as a divine signal, so the image was installed in the town, where it remained for some time, before continuing to its perch in Bangkok's Grand Palace (see p.23).

CHIANG RAI

The most exciting way of arriving in Chiang Rai, the city 180km (120 miles) to the north of Chiang Mai, is not by the route through the hills, nor by the 45-minute flight, but by the least comfortable option of the

*B*eautiful mountain scenery and abundant rivers in the north, around Tha Thon.

river boat from the town of Tha Thon. This is a trip for the adventurous – the boats are both small and narrow, with no toilets, while the engine is as loud (but not as powerful) as an aeroplane. Nonetheless, it is worth the effort, for the views on the 4-hour journey are quite simply spectacular.

Chiang Rai is mainly of use as a base from where to visit regional attractions, and you'll need to travel a short way out of this undistinguished town in order to see them. King Mengrai founded Chiang Rai in the 13th century, by chance so it is said. According to legend, his elephant ran off and led him to a spot on the Mae Kok River, where the scenery and military potential of the place inspired him to build a town. In recent years, town planners have unfortunately seen fit to fill it up with car showrooms and ugly concrete buildings.

Still, there are two temples worth a visit. At **Wat Phra Kaeo**, you can see another former home of the Emerald Buddha (see p.25 and above), the country's most famous image.

*A*kha girls in traditional costume pose for photographs on the bridge to Burma at Mae Sai.

At the Burmese-style **Wat Doi Tong**, you have the bonus of views of the river below and a glimpse of the town's old part.

Travel agencies in Chiang Rai operate excursions to the famous, hillside temple of **Doi Tung**, perched some 2,000m (2,188yd) up the mountain. On the way there you will pass the Queen Mother's summer residence and a royal-sponsored agricultural project, which is designed to help the hill tribes integrate into normal life. The tribespeople are encouraged to grow strawberries, cucumbers and cabbages in lieu of opium and in return receive government schools, new roads – and tourists who come here to purchase their wares.

Smaller tribal villages can also still be found in the mountains north of Chiang Rai and the area around Mae Chan. Be warned, however: pigs, water

62

buffalo and dogs may still burrow picturesquely among the stilt houses, but modern life has not passed by unnoticed, and the children of the tribespeople will ask for coins or, increasingly, notes. Even among the Yao villages of adobe huts with thatched roofs, many elders have learnt a few English words. The women, in red collared jackets and blue turbans, are usually more interested in selling handicrafts than telling of the Yao's origins in Southern China over 200 years ago.

Mae Sai and Chiang Saen

You can't go further north than Mae Sai, unless you take the footbridge across the Sai River into Burma. This charming little backwater with a sprinkling of markets and guesthouses is a good lunchtime spot on the way to the Golden Triangle.

Get there between 6am and 6pm and you'll see authorized travellers from Burma crossing the border into Thailand to sell products which they bring

Beautiful but deadly – opium from the poppies in Chiang Rai province is used to make heroin.

in by hand: cheroots, packaged prunes, ivory carvings, lacquer boxes, oranges and, more discreetly, items like gems and contraband cigarettes.

In the market take your pick from the wonderful Burmese puppets and tapestries known **64** as *kalaga*, or pay your Bt10 to photograph children dressed in hill tribe costume. If you're in luck, you may go to the end of the bridge to purchase strange Burmese vegetables or more innocuous local products.

From Mae Sai, tours usually continue the 12km (7 miles) to the infamous Golden Triangle, which forms a three-way border between Burma, Laos and Thailand. This spot, like many others, once saw huge quantities of opium being sent across the border, destined for heroin traders in Paris and New York.

A Selection
of Thai
Hotels and
Restaurants

Recommended Hotels

Below is a selection of hotels listed according to town or area, alphabetically. Prices will inevitably vary according to the season in which you visit, travel agent's package and unpredictable inflation. All the hotels included have air-conditioning. The following symbols are a basic guide to room prices (based on double occupancy with bath, but not including breakfast):

▌	Bt500–1,000 (Budget)
▌▌	Bt1,000–2,000 (Tourist)
▌▌▌	Over Bt2,000 (First Class)

BANGKOK
Local dialling code (02)

Comfort Inn ▌
Soi 11, Sukhumvit Road
Tel. 251 9250
Modern, no-frills hotel with fairly small rooms and a quiet but central location.

Dusit Thani ▌▌▌
946 Rama IV Road
Tel. 236 0450
One of Bangkok's most luxurious and tasteful hotels, offering excellent restaurants, swimming pool, and all the high-quality services you'd expect from a top rate establishment. 525 rooms.

Federal Hotel ▌
27 Soi 11, Sukhumvit Road
Tel. 253 0175/6
Welcoming, modern hotel with a swimming pool, patio and coffee shop. 80 rooms.

Impala Hotel ▌▌
9 Soi 24, Sukhumvit Road
Tel. 259 0053/4
Situated a little bit away from it all, and offering a swimming pool, sauna and health club amongst its facilities. 200 rooms.

Malaysia Hotel ▌
54 Soi Ngam Dupli,
Rama IV Road
Tel. 287 1457/8
Something like an upmarket backpackers' paradise, complete with a nearby pool and notorious 24-hour coffee shop. 120 rooms.

Manohra Hotel ▌▌
412 Surawong Road
Tel. 234 5070/89
Situated within walking distance of the Chao Phya River. All rooms have recently been renovated and there is an indoor swimming pool, cocktail lounge and pleasant roof garden. 250 rooms.

Menam Hotel   ▯▯▯
2074 Charoen Krung Road,
Yannawa
Tel. 289 1148/9 or 289 0352/3
The least expensive and most un-pretentious of the riverside hotels, with a swimming pool, health club and terraces. 727 rooms.

Opera Hotel   ▯
16 Soi 1, Phetchburi Rd.
Tel. 252 4031/2
Cheap, cheerful and popular, with pool and 24-hour coffee shop.

Oriental Hotel   ▯▯▯
48 Oriental Avenue,
Charoen Krung Road
Tel. 236 0400/0420
Nominated as one of the world's finest hotels, with two swimming pools, a host of famous clients and fine views of the river. 394 rooms.

Park Hotel   ▯▯
6 Soi 7, Sukhumvit Road
Tel. 255 4300/252 5110/3
Recently refurbished with swim-ming pool, fitness centre, sauna and jacuzzi. 139 rooms.

Royal Hotel   ▯▯
2 Ratchadamnoen Klang Road
Tel. 222 9111/20
One of Bangkok's venerable old institutions, positioned close to the famous Grand Palace. 300 rooms.

Shangri-La Hotel   ▯▯▯
89 Soi Wat Suan Plu,
Charoen Krung Road
Tel. 236 7777
A luxury establishment known for superb river views and fine restau-rants, and which offers a pool and top-class service. 694 rooms.

YMCA Collins
International House   ▯▯
27 Sathorn Road
Tel. 287 1900
Clean, friendly accommodation of a high standard, with a good value restaurant and adjacent swimming pool. 50 rooms.

CHIANG MAI
Local dialling code (053)

Chiang Mai Orchid   ▯▯▯
100 Huey Kaew Road
Tel. 222 099/222 091/3
One of Chiang Mai's best estab-lishments, with a swimming pool, fitness centre, nightclub and lively disco. 450 rooms.

Chiang Mai Plaza   ▯▯▯
92 Sri Donchai Road
Tel. 270 036/050
Offering all the facilities of a top international-class hotel and the convenience of a downtown loca-tion, with a large swimming pool and a popular disco. 450 rooms.   **67**

Galore Guest House
91 Charoenprathet Road
Tel. 249 088
An upmarket guesthouse in a charming situation overlooking the river, a short walk from town. 30 rooms.

Holiday Garden Hotel
16/16 Huey Kaew Road
Tel. 210 901
Located in downtown Chiang Mai, this peaceful family hotel is positioned around a courtyard with a swimming pool.

Hotel Top North Centre
41 Moonmuang Road
Tel. 213 309
Popular middle-of-the-road hotel, situated in a quiet cul-de-sac off Tapei Gate and within easy walk of a number of bars and temples.

Lai Thai Guest House
111/4–5 Kotchasarn Road
Tel. 251 689
A clean and modern, chalet-style hotel built around a courtyard, and with friendly staff. 90 rooms.

Once Upon a Time
385/2 Charoenprathet Road
Tel. 274 932
This hotel provides eccentric wooden rooms and is situated in beautifully exotic gardens.

Rim Ping Garden
411 Charoenprathet Road
Tel. 281 050/60
In an idyllic riverside setting, with a swimming pool, fine restaurant. and balconied rooms. 20 rooms.

Riverview Lodge
25 Soi 2, Charoenprathet Road
Tel. 271 110
Charming riverbank setting, with large garden and fine views. 36 rooms.

Royal Princess Hotel
112 Changklan Road
Tel. 281 033
Bright and elegant, with a swimming pool. Central location near the night market. 200 rooms.

CHIANG RAI
Local dialling code (053)

Dusit Island Resort
Maekok Villa,
1129 Kraisorasit Road
Tel. 711 786
Big international hotel with fine river views and excellent facilities.

Golden Triangle Inn
590 Phaholyothin Road
Tel. 711 339
In a quiet location near the heart of town. Charming staff and an excellent café.

Maekok Villa

445 Singhakai Road
Tel. 711 786
Charming bungalow-style rooms with bath and hot water, situated on the edge of town. 44 rooms.

Rama Hotel

34/1 Trairat Road
Tel. 711 344
Standard, centrally located hotel with coffee shop and a pub called 'Cheers'. 43 rooms.

Rimkok Resort

6 Mu 4, Tha Thon Road
Tel. 716 445/60
Massive hotel complex with jogging facilities, pool and fine river views. Sited approximately 5km (3 miles) from town. 248 rooms.

Wang Din Place

34/1 Kwae Wai Road
Tel. 713 363
Twelve comfortable riverside huts, 2km (1 mile) from town.

HAT YAI

Local dialling code (074)

JB Hotel

99 Juti Anusorn Road
Tel. 234 300/28
Tastefully decorated hotel with a swimming pool, tennis court and health club. 212 rooms.

King's Hotel

126-8 Niphat Uthit 1 Road
Tel. 243 966
Down-to-earth hotel in a central location, with cocktail lounge and coffee shop. 88 rooms.

Regency Hotel

23 Prachathipat Road
Tel. 234 400/9
Elegantly furnished in a central location, but no pool. 190 rooms.

HUA HIN

Local dialling code (032)

Hua Hin Highland Resort

Phetkasem Road
Tel. Bangkok 211 2579
Situated to the north of town, near the golf course. 13 rooms.

Royal Garden Resort

107/1 Phetkasem Road
Tel. 511 881/4
Offering a swimming pool, roof terrace, tennis courts, and even a view of the sea from every one of its 217 rooms.

Sailom

29 Phetkasem Road
Tel. 511 890/1
A popular upmarket hotel with a swimming pool and tennis courts. 60 rooms.

69

Sofitel Central   ▯▯▯
1 Damnoen Kasem Road
Tel. 512 021/30
A charming, colonial-style hotel positioned right on the beachfront and recently renovated to the highest standards. 218 rooms.

KANCHANABURI
Local dialling code (034)

Kasem Island Resort   ▯
27 Chaichumphon Road
Tel. 511 359
A selection of chalet-style rooms situated on an island in the Mae Klong River, with a good location – only a stone's throw away from Kanchanaburi town.

Pung Waan Resort   ▯▯
123/1 Tarsao, Sai Yok,
Kanchanaburi
Tel. Bangkok 591 017/8
A choice of either floating houses or brick huts situated a short way out of Kanchanaburi, and offering their own extensive and beautiful landscaped gardens, as well as a swimming pool.

River Kwai Hotel   ▯▯
284/3–16 Saeng Chuto Road
Tel. 511 184/269
Centrally located with a restaurant and swimming pool, but no views of the river. 127 rooms.

River Kwai Village   ▯▯
72 moo 2, Tarsao, Sai Yok,
Kanchanaburi
Tel. Bangkok 251 7522/7828
Situated to the west of town near the Sai Yok National Park, and offering diverse attractions – from a swimming pool and an abundance of package tours to a mini-zoo.

Sam's Place   ▯
Song Kwai Road
Tel. 513 971
Simple but charming river bungalows in a convenient location near to the main concentration of bars and floating restaurants.

KO SAMUI
Local dialling code (077)

Imperial Boat House Hotel   ▯▯▯
Choeng Mong Beach
Tel. 421 451/460
One of Ko Samui's most stunning developments, this hotel is made up of old teak canal barges which have been converted into luxury, land-based suites.

Chaweng Garden   ▯
Chaweng Beach
Tel. 421 403
Pretty bungalows made of wood in a leafy setting, close to the popular centre of Chaweng Beach.

Coral Bay Resort ▯▯
Bo Phut Beach
Tel. 422 223/4
Large, thatched bungalows with spacious balconies, plus a swimming pool and terrace.

Imperial Ko Samui ▯▯▯
Chaweng Beach
Tel. 421 390/7
International-class hotel, charmingly situated in a secluded cove, with beautiful gardens, two swimming pools and fine views.

Imperial's Tong Sai Bay Hotel ▯▯▯
Choeng Mong Beach
Tel. 425 015/24
International-class hotel built on the cliffs with Mediterranean-style balconies, a tennis court, private beach, swimming pool and spectacular views.

The Island ▯▯
Chaweng Beach
Tel. 230 941
Thatched bungalows, bar, restaurant and swimming pool situated on popular Chaweng Beach.

Matlang Resort ▯
Chaweng Beach
Tel. 272 222
At the quieter, northern end of Chaweng, set in a pretty garden.

PS Villa ▯
Choen Mong
Tel. 286 956
Clean and friendly, situated on a quiet beach with fine views.

Sandy Resort ▯
Bo Phut Beach
Tel. 425 353/4
Inland bungalows with a charming wooden terrace – the perfect spot to enjoy sundowners.

MAE HONG SON
Local dialling code (053)

Baiyoke Chalet ▯▯
90 Khunlumprapas Road
Tel. 611 486
Upmarket and with a central location, this chalet-style hotel offers cosy rooms and a restaurant.

Holiday Inn ▯▯▯
114/5-7 Khunlumprapas Road
Tel. 612 324
Big international-class hotel with a swimming pool, disco, bars, tour agency and convention facilities. 114 rooms.

Mae Hong Son Resort ▯
24 Ban Huey Dua
Tel. 611 406
Charming bungalows located 5km (3 miles) outside Mae Hong Son. 40 bungalows available.

71

Rim Nam Klang Doi Resort

Ban Huay Dua
Tel. 611 086
Standard and luxury huts on the river bank, 5km (3 miles) out of town, with a restaurant terrace and friendly staff.

Tara Mae Hong Son

149 Mu 8
Tel. 611 473
A five-star luxury hotel set in its own extensive landscaped gardens and with charming views. Offering a full range of facilities, including restaurants, tour agency and swimming pool.

PATTAYA

Local dialling code (038)

Diana Inn

216/6-7 Mu 9, Pattaya 2 Road
Tel. 429 675
Pleasant little hotel with a swimming pool, situated near the centre of town. 59 rooms.

Dusit Resort

240/2 Beach Road
Tel. 429 901/3
International-class hotel with good service and a wide choice of facilities, including a swimming pool, tennis courts and an opulent bar for evening drinks. 500 rooms.

Garden Lodge

Mu 5 Naklua Road
Tel. 429 109
Swimming pool and breakfast buffet. 58 rooms.

Ocean View Hotel

10 Beach Road
Tel. 428 084
Standard hotel overlooking Beach Road with a swimming pool, terrace and countless bars and restaurants nearby. 112 rooms.

PK Villa

Beach Road
Tel. 429 107
Always one of Pattaya's most popular establishments, set in a villa with well tended gardens and a swimming pool.

Royal Cliff Beach

Cliff Road, South Pattaya
Tel. 421 421/430
Considered by most to be the best hotel in town, with private beach, swimming pools, restaurants and exquisite views. 700 rooms.

Seaview Resort

Naklua Soi 20
Tel. 429 317
Situated away from it all, a short distance from North Pattaya, with a private beach, good swimming water and restaurant. 80 cottages.

Siam Bayshore   ▯▯▯
Beach Road
Tel. 428 678/81
Luxury hotel set in 8ha (20 acres) of woods and lovely tropical gardens, with a good location just a short walk from the busiest area of town. 265 rooms.

PHUKET
Local dialling code (076)

Amanpuri   ▯▯▯
118 Srisoonthorn Road,
Pansea Beach
Tel. 324 333
Phuket's finest hotel, with exclusive bungalows overlooking a secluded bay. Offering a swimming pool, tennis courts and a private cruiser. 40 rooms.

Boathouse Inn   ▯▯▯
Kata Beach
Tel. 330 557
A charming inn modelled on traditional Thai boathouses, offering a swimming pool, good restaurant and beachfront location.

Casuarina Bungalows ▯▯▯
Patong Beach
Tel. 340 123
Simple bungalows attractively set in pretty gardens, in a convenient location for Phuket's busiest and most exciting beach area.

Club Andaman   ▯▯
77/1 Patong Beach
Tel. 340 530
A choice of Thai-style thatched bungalows with a swimming pool and extensive landscaped gardens, near busy Patong.

Jungle Beach Resort   ▯▯
11/3 Vised Road, Nai Harn
Tel. 381 108 or 214 291
Attractively set in its own rocky bay, with swimming pool and terrace; one of the less developed areas of the island. 38 rooms.

Pansea Phuket Bay   ▯▯▯
Pansea Beach
Tel. 324 017/020
Luxurious thatched bungalows on stilts, plus a swimming pool, fine restaurant, good service, bars, terrace and private beach. 100 rooms.

Patong Beach Bungalow   ▯▯
96/1 Patong Beach
Tel. 340 117/340 213
Close to busy Patong, small swimming pool plus a beachfront terrace. 34 rooms.

Sunset Bungalows   ▯
Nai Harn Beach
Old-style beach bungalows ranged up the hillside in one of the least developed parts of the island.

73

Recommended Restaurants

Below is a selection of some of the eating establishments that have made Thailand a gastronomic delight, and in which we appreciated the food and service; if you find other places worth recommending, we would be pleased to hear from you. Our choices concentrate mainly on restaurants serving local cuisine, rather than international or Western. Some establishments close one day a week, which may vary, so it's often best to telephone ahead. Alternatively, just watch where the locals go and take your pick. You're unlikely to be disappointed.

Apart from the more expensive hotel restaurants, average meal prices (two dishes, rice and dessert) are fairly uniform – ranging from roughly Bt100 to Bt400 per adult. Beer is extra, of course, while wine for the most part is extremely expensive, sometimes even costing more than the meal. Restaurant opening hours are usually 11am-2pm and 6-10pm; some remain open all day. The following symbols are a guide to prices:

	cheap
	medium
	expensive

BANGKOK

Baan Khanitha

36/1 Sukhumvit Soi 23
High-quality Thai cuisine in an elegant and traditional Thai house.

Baan Thai

7 Soi 32, Sukhumvit Road
Tel. 258 5403
A diverse selection of Thai dishes modified for the Western palate, accompanied by classical dancing. Nightly performances are from 7.30 to 10pm.

Ban Khrua

29/1 Soi Saladaeng 1
Silom Road
Tel. 233 6912
Simple but comfortable restaurant, with good local specialities on the menu.

Bussaracum

35 Soi 2 Piphat
Convent Road
Tel. 235 8915
Authentic Thai cuisine, featuring *sakunna chom suan* (shrimp birds with taro).

The China House   III
Oriental Hotel,
48 Oriental Avenue
Tel. 236 0400
Bangkok's first and finest classic Cantonese restaurant, situated in an elegant wooden house. The excellent food includes shark's fin soup and roast pigeon stuffed with herbs. This restaurant is expensive compared to normal Bangkok standards.

China Restaurant   II
231/3 Soi Sarasin
Tel. 251 0737/8
Szechuan, Cantonese, Mandarin, Shanghai and a selection of other Chinese regional dishes on the menu.

Jade Garden   II
Montien Hotel,
54 Surawong Road
Tel. 233 7060
Popular Cantonese cuisine, particularly the *dim sum*, as well as delicious noodles, steamed dumplings and Peking duck.

La Banane   II
99/24 Langsuan Balcony
Ploenchit Road
Tel. 251 9822
Friendly atmosphere. Good value Thai cuisine with an emphasis on seafood.

Lemon Grass   II
5/1 Soi 24, Sukhumvit Road
Tel. 258 8637
Set in a delightful old house with a charming terrace. Excellent Thai food, but the portions are on the small side.

Loy Nava Floating Restaurant   II
Reached from River City Pier
Tel. 437 4932
Departs every evening for a dinner cruise on Bangkok's Chao Phya, River, serving good Western and European food. Advance booking is recommended.

Madame Cherie   I
Charn Issara Tower,
Rama IV Road
Tel. 234 2211
Popular Vietnamese cuisine located near Bangkok's red-light district.

Maharaj   I
22/5-7 Maharaj Road
Tel. 221 4389
Situated upriver from the Grand Palace. Get there by sundown and feast on the excellent curries and spicy *tom yam kung* (prawn soup).

Patara   I
1/2 Sukhumvit Soi 26
Tel. 261 0336

75

Cosy restaurant serving fine Thai cuisine at medium-level cost.

Royal India Restaurant

392/1 Chakraphet Road
Tel. 221 6565
Small and extremely popular, with fine tandooris, Madras curries and Indian sweets.

Sala Rim Naam
Oriental Hotel

48 Oriental Avenue,
Charoen Krung Road
Tel. 437 9417
Set in a charming location on the banks of the Chao Phya River, with exquisite classical dancing every night (at 8.30pm). Serving some of the best – and most expensive – Thai food to be found in the city.

Seafood Market

Soi 24, Sukhumvit Road
Choose your seafood in a shopping trolley, then sit outside and feast on some of the best fish and lobsters in town.

Silom Village

286 Silom Road
Tel. 234 4581
Fresh fish and Chinese and Thai specialities served at both open-air and indoor restaurants, to the accompaniment of Thai music.

Spice Market

The Regent Hotel,
155 Ratchadamri Road
Tel. 251 6127
Remembering the days of a forgotten era and capturing the feel of old Siam with fine seafoods, green curries and spicy *tom yam*.

Tam Nak Thai

131 Rachadapisek Road
Tel. 274 6420/22
The second largest restaurant in the world, seating up to an astounding 3,000 diners, who are attended not only by 120 chefs, but also 400 waiters on rollerskates!

Thanying Restaurant

10 Pramuan Street,
Off Silom Road
Tel. 236 4361
Beautifully presented Thai food in an upmarket and stylish renovated Thai house. Particularly worth trying is the wild pork, stir-fried with lesser galangal and basil, or alternatively the duck curry.

Whole Earth

93/3 Soi Lang Suan,
Ploenchit Road
Tel. 252 5574
One of Bangkok's only vegetarian restaurants, also offering a wide selection of non-vegetarian and Thai dishes.

CHIANG MAI

Antique House
71 Charoenprathet Road
Tel. 276 810
Thai and European cuisine in teak house with antiques gallery. Near night bazaar.

Ban Suan
51/3 Sankamhaeng Road
Tel. 242 116
Situated in several 100-year-old teakwood barns on the outskirts of town and serves a wide selection of Thai food.

Chiang Mai Cultural Centre
185/3 Wualai Road
Tel. 275 097
A set *khantoke* dinner, including specialities such as *nam prik ong* (minced pork with chillies).

Diamond Hotel
33/10 Charoenprathet Road
Tel. 234 155
A set *khantoke* meal accompanied by traditional dancing in an old teak house. Book in advance.

Gallery
25–29 Charoenrat Road
Tel. 248 601
Delicacies such as spicy curry and banana flower salad.

Kai Tong Restaurant
67 Kotchasarn Road
Tel. 276 584
Serves fried frog, monitor lizard and tortoise, and claims to be the only restaurant in the world with python steak on the menu.

Kaiwan Restaurant
181 Nimanhemin Road
Tel. 222 147
Attractively situated on a peaceful veranda. Especially recommended is the *kratongtong* pancake filled with chicken in white sauce.

La Villa Pizzeria
145 Ratchadamnoen Road
Tel. 215 403
Bright and friendly establishment famed for its seafood pizzas and ravishing antipasti.

Rajawadee Restaurant
411 Charoenprathet Road
Tel. 281 060
Riverside hotel restaurant specializing in a broad selection of Thai, European and Chinese dishes.

Riverside
9/11 Charoenrat Road
Tel. 243 239
Particularly popular in the early evening for its views of the river and later for rock bands, as well as its European and Thai cuisine.

Whole Earth Restaurant

88 Sridonchai Road
Tel. 282 463

A generous selection of vegetarian, non-vegetarian, Indian and Thai food is served in this northern-style house. Charming atmosphere.

CHIANG RAI

Dusit Island Café

1129 Kraisolrasit
Tel. 715 777

Here you will find a variety of northern specialities served on a pleasant terrace overlooking the river.

Golden Triangle Café

590 Phaholyothin Road
Tel. 711 339

Popular and friendly, serving delicious Thai, Chinese and Western food, and occasionally hosting a folk band.

HAT YAI

Best Kitchern

53 Juti Anusorn Road
Tel. 234 479

Bright and popular restaurant, with over 100 dishes on the menu, including a speciality of curried wild boar.

Hillman Restaurant

154–8 Niphat Uthit 3 Road
Tel. 244 333

Famous for its roast suckling pig and lemon chicken.

KO SAMUI

Imperial Samui Restaurant

Imperial Samui Hotel,
Chaweng Beach
Tel. 421 390

Delightfully situated, at one of the island's top hotels, with superlative, if expensive, Thai and European cuisine.

Imperial Tongsai Bay Restaurant

Imperial Tongsai Bay Hotel,
Ban Plailaem, Bophut
Tel. 421 451

Regarded by most as the *crème de la crème* of Ko Samui's cooking, with the advantage of being in one of its most beautiful settings. A perfect restaurant for celebrations.

PATTAYA

Dolf Ricks

Sri Nakorn Centre,
North Pattaya
Tel. 428 269

One of Pattaya's oldest and best-loved restaurants, with good-value

Indonesian and European food. The house speciality is a *rijstafel*, a combination of 18 dishes.

El Toro Steak House
215–31 Pattaya 2 Road
Tel. 426 238
For good old steaks, chips and crowds, nothing can beat the El Toro Steak House.

La Gritta
Beach Road
Tel. 428 161
Good, authentic Italian food. Try the pasta with clams, herbs and white wine. Book early.

Orchard Grill
Beach Road
Tel. 423 639
French and continental cuisine in a hotel restaurant.

Pattaya Seafood Palace
Mu 10
Tel. 427 396
Good lobster, mussels and freshly caught fish in a pleasant setting.

PIC Kitchen
Soi 5, Beach Road
Tel. 428 374
Delicious and widely acclaimed, some of the most authentic local Thai cuisine served in a charming atmosphere, surrounded by traditional architecture. Do not miss.

Ruen Thai Restaurant
Pattaya 2 Road, South Pattaya
Tel. 425 911
This Thai restaurant is set in beautiful gardens and serves fine curries and regional specialities. Meals are accompanied by exquisite classical dancing.

Tam Nak Nam
252 Central Road
Tel. 429 059
A Chinese-style seafood restaurant with barbecued fish, mussels and lobsters. Built on concrete pillars above a pond.

Thang Long
Soi 3, 201 Pattaya
Tel. 425 487
Classical Vietnamese food served by waitresses in traditional Vietnamese costume.

Villa Seafood Restaurant
Soi 7, Pattaya Beach Road
Tel. 422 523
At the Villa Seafood Restaurant original Chinese recipes are used in the preparation of specialities like stir-fried black pepper crabs, five-flavoured grilled king lobster, and Peking duck.

PHUKET

Ban Rim Pa III
100/7 Kalim Beach Road
Tel. 340 789
One of Phuket's finest restaurants, in a beautiful teak house, with excellent duck curry and *tom yam*.

Buffalo Steak House II
95/24–26 Soi Patong Resort
Tel. 340 855
This restaurant is known for its New Zealand beef steak, Scandinavian and German dishes, and even elephant's ear!

Malee Seafood II
Thawiwong Road
Patong Beach
Tel. 340 205
Seafood and steaks served in a beautiful indoor garden.

Phuket View Restaurant II
Khao Rang Hill
Tel. 216 865
Serving a wide range of fresh seafood, Thai and European dishes, and affording fine views.

Pizzeria Holiday Inn II
Patong Beach
Tel. 321 020
Pizzas from wood-fired brick oven served by pool in the garden.

Ruam Thep Inn I
Karon Beach
A popular seafood restaurant with a vast menu of Thai, Chinese and Western dishes.

Seafood Market I
Patong Night Plaza
Tel. 723 0566
Select your own seafood and watch it being cooked exactly how you like. Lively atmosphere.

Terrace Restaurant III
Amanpuri Hotel,
118 Srisoonthorn Road,
Pansea Beach
Tel. 311 394/9
One of the best restaurants you'll find on Phuket, serving top-of-the-range Thai cuisine.

Tung Ka Café II
Khao Rang Hill
Tel. 211 500
Delicious seafood curry served in coconut, glass noodles with crab and tempura shrimps – all accompanied by awesome views.

Vecchia Venezia II
82/16 U Thit Road,
Patong Beach
Italian fare with a Thai touch – choose your fish from the viewing tank or try other specialities such as homemade pasta and pizzas.

A Meo boy in Mae Hong Son province. The Meo are the most independent of the tribes.

Now, despite Thailand's estimated opium production of 30 tons a year, the figure is dropping, as a result of government encouragement to diversify into less sinister crops. Poppies won't be seen here, since discretion confines cultivation to the less accessible valleys, as well as to those vast areas in Burma which are controlled by the so-called 'opium armies' and the famous prince of poppies, Khun Sa.

A short drive west from Ban Sop Ruak will bring you to the friendly little town of Chiang Saen, set in a marvellous location on the gentle banks of the mighty Mekong River.

Despite its dilapidated feel, this town boasts a remarkably grand history. From the 10th to 13th centuries it was the seat of power for one of the earliest northern principalities – traces of this glorious past are scattered through what has since become a sleepy market town, where you can easily spend an afternoon exploring a moated city wall, Wat Phra That Chom Kitti – reputed to house part of Lord Buddha's forehead – the ruins of several other temples, and a museum showing Stone Age utensils and statues from Chiang Saen's golden era. Visitors who have more time for leisurely travelling will also be rewarded with timeless sunsets over the great Mekong River, and marvellous views of Laos, just a stone's throw away.

81

MAE HONG SON

December and January are the prime months to visit the town of Mae Hong Son, which lies squeezed between mountains 270km (168 miles) north west of Chiang Mai and is reached by a hair-raising but staggeringly beautiful eight-hour road trip or a less bumpy 30-minute flight. At this time of year, the sky is at its bluest, the winter flowers blossom, and the air is lush and cool. It doesn't really matter what month you come, however, for this city offers no shortage of attractions.

Until 1831, when an expedition was sent there by the king of Chiang Mai in search of the rare white elephant, Mae Hong Son's history was as misty as its valleys. The expedition was so successful, however, that a small settlement was founded, and by 1874 Mae Hong Son was a provincial capital.

Although you're unlikely to see wild elephants, what you will come across are Burmese-style temples standing on the banks of the Jongkhum Lake, and framed against the distant hills. Most people like exploring the market at dawn – when

The City of Mists, Mae Hong Son, has recently become fashionable, but retains its charm.

82

the hill tribe people in traditional dress can sometimes be seen buying vegetables – before going on any of the plethora of tours. Guides arrange elephant riding and river rafting, or will drive you to tribal villages at the Burmese border.

The sight of Padang's **'long-necked people'**, with necks as long as 30cm (12in), will not be to everyone's taste. Legend has it that the tribe's ancestors were a female dragon and the wind god, and it was in imitation of the image of the dragon that the women took up the unusual 'long-neck' tradition. Inevitably, the reality now is that this ungainly appearance helps attract tourists. Known as the 'Padang', this can be taken as meaning 'Giraffe People'.

In the area surrounding Mae Hong Son you have the chance to explore caves and waterfalls or merely breathe in the fresh air of the mountains (jeeps and motorbikes can both be hired). Keen drivers and bus passengers can return to Chiang Mai on a circular route that goes via Mae Sariang and Hot, so that towns visited previously are not repeated. Visitors who can't face another tortuous and winding eight-hour trip have the option of taking the plane.

Southern Thailand

Southern Thailand, stretching thinly down to Malaysia, gives you a choice of seas. The considerably longer eastern coast is on the familiar Gulf of Thailand, while the west is washed by the Indian Ocean. On either side, though, you'll find sensational beaches, while the land between – rice fields, coconut and rubber plantations – is as scenic as it is fertile. Planes fly to Phuket and Ko Samui from Bangkok; otherwise, there are trains and buses and the opportunity to explore several of the small, picturesque fishing villages along the way.

Korrekt Spelling

Thai signmakers often transliterate names into English, but with glorious inconsistency. Sometimes you see Petchburi, or often Petburi, Phetchburi or Phetburi. In the same way, the island of Phuket (pronounced poo-ket) can be spelt with rather unfortunate connotations. This underlines the difficulty of trying to speak Thai – a language with 48 vowels and 44 consonants, and which is fiendishly tonal: the word *ma* means 'horse', 'dog' or 'to come', depending on how it is pronounced.

PHUKET

Phuket (pronounced poo-ket) is Thailand's top beach destination, with some of the most beautiful beaches and luxurious hotels in the land, in addition to sailing, snorkelling and an abundance of nightlife.

Covering around 810sq km (315sq miles) and made up of a mountainous interior which,

until recently, was the site of tin mines, Phuket offers over a dozen white-sand beaches, as well as national parks, inland plantations and waterfalls.

It attracts over one million tourists every year – almost six times the island's total population – most of whom arrive by plane (55 minutes from Bangkok), although tourist coaches also do the journey in just over

With so many beautiful islands to choose from, no wonder Thai sailors are a happy-go-lucky bunch.

85

14 hours, crossing the causeway from the mainland.

Although Phuket has been transformed by the invasion of tourists, and new hotels are almost as abundant as water buffalo, you are nonetheless spoilt with some of the most beautiful scenery and clearest seas in the region.

Even historians might find something to interest them in Phuket. From the airport, the highway south goes through a dusty village called **Thalang**, the site of the island's ancient capital. Burmese invaders besieged, pillaged and destroyed Thalang in 1809.

In an earlier and more positive chapter of history, the city managed to withstand a siege by the Burmese which went on for longer than a month. This battle in 1786 led to both Lady Muk and her sister Lady Chan being regarded as heroines, for taking command of the town's defence following the death of Lady Muk's husband, the governor. Statues of these short-haired, women warriors, with full honours, stand in a traffic **86** circle down the road.

The new capital, also called Phuket or Phuket Town, is not so much a sight in its own right as more of a departure and arrival point. A couple of streets of traditional Sino-Portuguese, two-storey houses have been preserved, and a host of shopping centres, cafés and excellent seafood restaurants can be found. Souvenir shops still sell coral, wonderful seashells and locally cultivated – and counterfeited – pearls.

Most visitors, however, find it hard to tear themselves away from the sun and sea. Watersports of all kinds are offered, from waterskiing to paragliding, and windsurfers, catamarans and yachts can be hired. Fresh seafood makes for memorable meals, and everyone at some stage treats themselves to the famous Phuket lobster, which is best eaten grilled and with a dash of lime.

Beaches and Islands

The best beaches are on the west coast of the island, where fine, white sand slopes slowly into the Andaman Sea (Indian Ocean) . **Patong** beach, 15km (9 miles) west of Phuket Town by paved road, is the island's most beautiful and most developed, packed with bungalows,

*P*atong Beach on Phuket is paradise to anyone from colder climes, but it's not the best place for peace and quiet.

hotels, restaurants, bars, pubs and discos.

The marvellous beaches of **Kata** and **Karon** are less developed, though rapid building has provided an abundance of tasteful family resorts offering every comfort. More secluded is **Pansea**, home to the Amanpuri and Pansea Hotels, two of the quietest and most exclusive addresses on the island. A bit further south at Nai Harn, you will find some of Phuket's last beach bungalows, squeezed in between two rocky headlands.

It is possible to hire a jeep to tour the island, but be warned that some roads are steep and accidents not uncommon. The most dramatic viewing point is the **Laem Promthep** promontory, which is 19km (12 miles) south west of Phuket Town. A single palm stands majestically, ready to frame the sunset, keeping photographers happy.

The sea views from Phuket are dotted with 30 or so uninhabited islands, to which owners of long-tailed boats operate excursions from some beaches for picnics and/or snorkellling. Local experts say the grounds

for scuba diving are first rate, with plenty of coral and brilliantly hued fish. Even better are the Similan Islands, which have national marine park status. Deep-sea expeditions can be arranged to catch mackerel, barracuda and sailfish.

EXCURSIONS FROM PHUKET

Phuket travel agencies offer a variety of day-long excursions. Anyone who knows the James Bond film, *The Man with the Golden Gun*, will not want to miss out **Phang Nga**, where the bay contains the superb, mushroom-shaped rock formations featured in the film, and which still lure holidaymakers with their exotic appeal. Long-tailed boats skim through the mangrove into a dreamscape of mad mountain tops, and at two points of the journey sail through tunnels worn beneath limestone islands by the tides.

On the way they will stop at **Panyi** island, where the Muslim fishing people have built a village on stilts above the sea and now enjoy the attention of thousands of tourists, who buy their woodwork and fresh fish.

The real highlight, though, is **Ko Tapu** (meaning literally nail island), which was formed thousands of years ago as a result of some fantastical earthquake. The island rises straight up out of the water to a height of 200m (656ft).

Adventurers can escape the crowds by hiring boats to more distant, uninhabited islands – although make sure that before leaving you agree on the price and the number of islands that you will be visiting.

A separate excursion is offered to the beautiful **Phi Phi islands**. Boats go from Phuket

An underground cave at Phang Nga, the spectacular, limestone-studded bay east of Phuket.

When the gods made Thailand, they sprinkled it liberally with sparkling white beaches and islands, turquoise seas and crystal sands.

daily and the trip south lasts two hours. Day tours will take you to the Viking Cave and to beautiful Maya Bay. Do spend a night there if possible, so you will have time to enjoy some of the most incredible scenery in the country. Underwater enthusiasts can explore some of the richest marine life found in the Andaman. Fish are not the only attraction, either, for high up in the sea cliffs lives a vast number of sea swallows. The nests that the birds build so industriously at great heights are collected at considerable risk by the islanders – it's a profitable export business, supplying Chinese restaurants with the raw material for that great, but expensive delicacy – bird's nest soup. Locals believe that the soup will provide a cure for skin and lung problems as well as impotence and loss of appetite. Such is the demand that some nests fetch prices as high as 1,000 US dollars.

Closer to Phuket – and considerably cheaper – is the popular **Naga Noi Pearl Farm**, which can be visited by half-day excursion. This is home to the biggest cultivated pearl in the world, weighing a massive 30g (1oz). Boats carry groups of tourists to the island daily to watch the pearl cultivation and after lunch will drop you back at your hotel.

☑ KO SAMUI

Backpackers long ago thought that they could keep Ko Samui secret. However, this tropical, palm-fringed island, just three hours from Surat Thani, has become one of the best-known havens in the south, with idyllic hotels and bungalows and even an airport. Not that it has necessarily spoilt the laid-back feel of the place, for people are still coming here to laze on the beaches, eat excellent seafood, visit the surrounding islands –

and most of all just to get away from the hustle and bustle.

Honeymooners and comfort seekers often stay on Chaweng Beach, which is arguably the most beautiful stretch, packed with restaurants and discos. If you want something more exclusive, try peaceful Choengmon Beach. For the pick of the cheaper hotels and bungalows, head for Lamai to the south.

A host of beach sports is offered, as well as tennis, waterfall trips and even an excursion to a coconut-picking farm. For an afternoon trip, you can also rent a motorcycle or jeep and go on a tour of the island. The road follows the coast almost right the way round, though you should stop off at Lamai to visit the intriguing museum and see the odd-shaped rocks known universally as 'grandfather rocks'. Remember that the roads are steep though – and tourists with grazed knees are by no means an uncommon sight. A safer means of transport is a *songthaew*, but they only run until 6pm.

There are daily flights from Bangkok to Ko Samui, taking **91** just 50 minutes. Buses take 15 hours, while trains run to Surat Thani, from where it is two hours by boat to Ko Samui.

HAT YAI

More than two-thirds of the way down the southern coast, and half an hour's drive inland, you will come to a town best known for sex and smuggling. Hat Yai is the fastest-growing provincial capital in the country, and as such has to deal with the crowds of Malaysians who cross the border daily for cheap shopping and sinning.

Visit the market off Niphat Uthit Road, where local goods and electrical items are sold. More interesting are the snake stalls, where you can drink a pint of snakes' blood, mixed with a little alcohol or honey. At **Wat Hat Yai** you can get right into the abdomen of a giant reclining Buddha to explore the sculpted heart and lungs, which are said to hold a relic of the Buddha.

An exotic daytime attraction can be watched on the first or second Sunday of each month:

bullfighting Thai style. In this, Thai bulls lock horns in a tenacious struggle for superiority, and the slightest indication of movement animates the audience. Gamblers, who make up the vast majority of the crowd, explode in yells of encouragement, until a combatant sends a silent signal of surrender and backs away. Visitors with no sporting interest in these proceedings will find eight hours a bit much, but it's worth staying for one or two matches.

SONGKHLA

Although Songkhla has never been known for its nightlife, this sleepy town – which is situated 30km (18 miles) northeast of Hat Yai and is the very antithesis of its neighbour – offers a wide range of other attractions, amongst them lakes, beaches and grand ramparts.

Quiet, dignified and charming, Songkhla has a surprising history of colour and intrigue. For centuries it was an important commercial centre, part of the strong Srivijaya kingdom which ruled much of maritime

South East Asia, but in 1654 it declared itself an independent state from Ayutthaya. Its independence didn't last, however, for in 1679 King Narai the Great of Ayutthaya left the place virtually abandoned having attacked it with cannons.

Even though the white sand here goes on for miles, swimming is not good and the season is short. It's better to walk along the shady waterfront or to indulge in a picnic at the outdoor seafood restaurants.

On the far side of the peninsula, where Thailand's biggest lake meets the sea, the port of Songkhla is as colourful as its red, blue and green trawlers. You can watch these landing giant prawns, then follow the seafood to market.

For cultural interest, try the National Museum, which is over a century old and houses collections of local archaeological finds, old furniture and items from the prehistoric site of Ban Chiang. Also, on Red Mountain, parts of the old fort with 18 turrets can be seen.

Ornithologists will want to see one of southern Thailand's greatest bird parks, though this entails a 2-hour journey north of town in order to get there. More than 100 different bird species can be found at **Khu Khut**, including a variety of ducks and kingfishers. The way to see them is by renting long-tailed boats. It is best to go during the early morning or late afternoon, since during the middle of the day you will be roasted by the heat.

*B*irds play hide-and-seek in and out of the water flowers in Songkhla province.

✓ Angkor Wat (Cambodia)

An hour and a quarter's flight from Bangkok will get you to one of the great wonders of the world. Angkor Wat, about 800 years old, is more than just another temple; it is a vast and spectacular work of art which stands as a monument to the unforgettable achievements of a distant civilization.

To get there you will have to change plane in the Cambodian capital of Phnom Penh (and put up with the uncertainties of the local airline); still, the rewards of such a trip are worth any delays.

It was Henri Mouhot, the 19th-century French naturalist who first discovered the glories of Angkor, when exploring the country as part of a trip which also took in Siam and Laos. Up until a few years ago, the site was cut off by wars and instability. Now it can be visited once again, though it is advisable to enquire about the situation with travel agents some weeks prior to departure.

Most tours will begin at the French-colonial-style town of Siem Reap, with its spattering of markets, hotels and restaurants. From here it's just a 20-minute bus ride to the fabled towers of Angkor Wat, which are visible above the treetops.

Before looking around the sprawling, ancient capital, you will probably go to **Angkor Thom**, a 12th-century, walled and moated city. The entrance used by the bus is one of five ceremonial gates that are overlooked by huge stone faces of the Compassionate Bodhisattva, a deity of one of the Buddhist sects. At the very centre of the enclave is the **Bayon**, a temple so big that, as you explore it, you are liable to end up by yourself, with nobody for company but the awesome face of an idol. Bas-reliefs and voluptuous statues are among the details that have survived invasions and the elements.

Angkor Thom also contains the **Terrace of the Elephants**, where stone bas-reliefs depict elephants at peace and war. An elegant, stone causeway, wide enough for a parade, leads to

Angkor Wat – the most imposing monument of the capital of the Khmer Empire.

the main gate of **Angkor Wat**, a royal mausoleum built by the Khmer Suryavarman II, who reigned from 1113 to 1150. Its splendid galleries, courtyards, halls and pavilions are beyond expectation. You can climb to the top of the central pyramid and look down over the entire establishment, then study in detail the intricate, sandstone carvings, with their powerful Khmer images of the Buddha and other deities.

Every corner, every flight of steps, reveals a new perspective. Wander through the cool, quiet cloisters which could belong to a Mediterranean monastery, reflect on the creative power which inspired so great an edifice, or simply watch the sun as it sets above the vast lotus ponds and the mass of the surrounding jungle.

95

What to Do

Thailand offers an unbeatable choice of indoor and outdoor activities, even if the heat is such that sometimes all you want is a swim. From classical dance to Thai boxing matches, or deep-sea diving to bustling markets, the sheer variety open to visitors is simply incredible. Most TAT (Tourism Authority of Thailand) offices distribute leaflets which list details of the various activities. If you find you're lucky enough to be in Thailand at the time of a major festival, make sure that you don't miss one of the country's most joyous occasions.

Folklore

Forget the fairies and demons. It's those traditional *manorha* dancers and wonderful, twanging instruments which are the nation's most prized gift from antiquity. You might be fortunate enough to see them at village fêtes or even at weddings and funerals, though nowdays

they are more common at special tourist shows, in which the highlights are condensed and explained. Such performances are usually accompanied by a banquet of Thai food, which renders the experience doubly pleasant. These special spectacles often feature the northern 'fingernail dance', in which an eloquent expression of epic tales is conveyed by a dancer wearing golden fingernails.

Wearing classical or peasant costumes, the same performers may then come back to enact hilltribe, war, sword and harvest dances.

Thai martial arts performed at these tourist shows include battles using sharp swords and sticks. The ritual which should always precede the bout involves the fighters kneeling to pay homage to their instructors and to invoke the help of the spirits, all done to the accompaniment of oboes and drums.

Exquisite movement: graceful Thai dance was traditionally only performed in front of kings.

Sports

In Thailand's tropical swelter it would be madness to exert oneself under the midday sun. Still, there are plenty of things to do, either as a participant or as an observer, and both the TAT and the local press detail activities as well as useful contact numbers.

Watersports

With some of the most beautiful waters in the Far East, it is little wonder that Thailand has become a beacher's paradise.

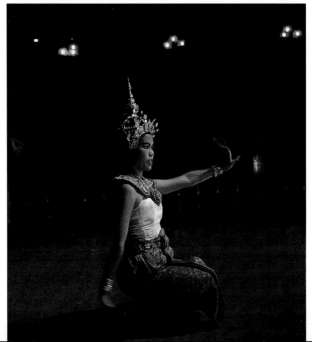

97

Once you have finished sunning yourself, though, there is no shortage of other activities.

Sailboats are available for hire at various beaches, as are other types of vehicles, such as pedal boats and speedy little water scooters.

Fishing has only been exploited recently as a sport in Thailand, but now Bang Sare has become something of the 'headquarters', although good catches of sailfish, marlin and shark have been made by several specialists in Pattaya. If all you want is a day relaxing on deck with a rod to tempt snapper, mackerel or parrotfish, it can easily be arranged.

Scuba diving is practised at most of the major resorts, and lessons are also offered. If you have five days to devote to it, you can progress from beginner to internationally certified undersea diver.

Water-ski fans will find the required equipment and powerful boats at popular beaches.

Windsurfing requires great coordination, but worthwhile instruction is offered (allow 15 hours for a diploma).

Other Sports

If you prefer to keep your feet on the shore, there are plenty of other sports to consider.

Tennis courts are found in almost all the big hotels, as are fitness centres and swimming pools (both in- and outdoors).

Horse-racing at Bangkok's two royal racetracks is held on most Saturdays and Sundays.

Golf lovers will soon realize that Thailand offers some fine golfing, with several top-class

*P*huket caters to all tastes when it comes to watersports; hire a jet foil and take off into the blue.

courses around Bangkok and Pattaya, and more being built in other tourist areas.

For the biggest knock-out sport, you just can't beat **Thai boxing**. This unique sport may be seen at folklore shows or at stadiums in Bangkok and other towns. Only kangaroos could outdo these agile punchers and kickers, who, as well as using gloved fists, fight with their elbows, knees and feet to battle it out. Good seats are quite expensive, while third-class seats offer the excitement of spirited betting, music and ritual. Get there early to take your pick.

Shopping

From the moment you reach Thailand you'll be astounded by the wealth of things to buy. Items range from stunning silk products to wooden bowls and silver earrings, from transportable goods such as textiles and clothes to fine woodwork and fragile, colourful pots. Whatever you want, Bangkok will provide you with something to fit the bill – with the notable exception of electronics, for which you would be better advised to visit Singapore.

Nor is Bangkok the only option. Chiang Mai is renowned for its handicrafts, while even the smaller towns in the northeast of the country boast their own specialities.

Tips for Shoppers

Remember that bargaining is the rule just about everywhere, apart from supermarkets and hotels – with even the large, upmarket boutiques occasionally being amenable to a little bit of negotiation.

Conversely, you should also keep it in mind that while fixed prices may sometimes be more expensive, they can still offer excellent value, and come with the added bonus of some form of guarantee. Sukhumvit Road in Bangkok is crammed with large, modern shopping plazas and department stores where there is no shortage of either imported or local offerings. It makes sense to wait to do your main shopping at the end of your holiday, so that you don't **99** have to carry it around with you – and you'll also have a better idea by then of what you want to take home.

In Bangkok, try to plan your shopping expeditions to avoid unnecessary travel, since traffic jams make travelling round the city time-consuming, hot and hazardous to your health.

Markets

Air-conditioned shops might sound like the best idea in the big cities, but it is the local markets that offer the real bargains. They are definitely worth a visit, if only to see the crowds and experience the joy and excitement of the Far East. Don't forget to bring a camera and to get there early, since many are like ghost towns by the middle of the day.

One of the biggest, most diverse and best known markets in Bangkok is the **Chatuchak Weekend Market** (see p.31). Fruit, vegetables and spices all vie for space with pastes and food concoctions you've probably never come across before. As for take-home curios, you

might like a brass temple bell, a carved buffalo horn, hilltribe embroidered clothing or handmade silver jewellery. You'll also find silk flowers, batik, a variety of modern T-shirts with startling, 'almost English' slogans, straw baskets and a mixture of oddities from Malaysia, India, Nepal and Burma.

The weekday equivalent of Chatuchak can be found at the Thieves Market, Pahurat and Chinatown, all located within easy reach of one another.

Chinatown is worth a visit simply for the sightseeing. The emphasis here is on goods with a Chinese flavour or origin, and one exotic possibility is to visit the perfume man, who'll make up a scent to please your nose while you wait.

The **Thieves Market** has a wide range of curios, some of them antique – remember, you need an export certificate for genuine items (see p.120).

For sumptious silks, clothing, cloth and delicate batiks, the bargains are to be found in **Pahurat Market**. Here, products from India and Malaysia are sold alongside local items.

Another market worth visiting is **Klong Toey Market**, where you'll find a wide range of culinary items, clothing and electrical goods at low prices.

Finally, if you like to combine your shopping with your nightlife, head for Patpong, the notorious red-light district. As well as private services for sale in discos and clubs, the streets are packed with stalls. A great many of the items for sale are 'genuine' imitations, including designer clothes, luggage, exclusive 'Rolex' watches and so on. Haggling is essential.

Best Buys

Antiques: if you qualify as an informed collector, then you'll find worthwhile objects from Thailand, Burma, China, Laos and Cambodia at the Thieves' Market, in smarter shops or in the provinces. Experts at the National Museum in Bangkok meet with the public on both Sundays and Mondays, when they vouch for the authenticity of works of art and antiquity. Don't forget – export permission is required for taking genuine antiques or art treasures out of the country (see p.120).

Art: paintings in several media by Thai artists, usually on familiar rice paddy or temple spire themes, are sold in galleries and shops all over the main towns. Temple stone rubbings on rice paper are another typical souvenir.

The Art of Bargaining

Want a natty wooden elephant, a lurid leather bag or even a ride in a taxi? Then remember to bargain for it. First ask how much the price is. Then name a figure considerably lower and somewhat less than you are prepared to pay, and eventually agree on a compromise. A few hints to help out: always check the prices on several stalls to get an idea of the cost; don't be misled by sweet smiles and sob stories – and remember, at the end of the day, so long as you are happy with the price then you've got a bargain.

Artificial flowers: as well as cultivating some of the world's most beautiful flowers, Thailand also exports large quantities of hand-made imitations.

Bronze: a great Thai tradition, which is now used for rust-free tableware in addition to lamps, bells, candelebra and statues.

Ceramics: a particular wood is used to fire the kilns to bake *celadon*, a distinctive Thai pottery. Porcelain is also made in Thailand. Ming and Ching dynasty bowls and shards turn up, salvaged from the river at Ayutthaya and Sukhothai; so do imitations.

Dolls: including hilltribe costumes, Thai dancers and peasant women in *sampans.*

Elephants: this favourite Thai symbol is often immortalized in wood carvings, thumb-sized to life-sized, jade and in flashy models studded with glass.

Fashion: clothes to order – allegedly in 24 hours or less – can be a solid bargain in Thailand, but try to give the tailor several days if you want a first-rate garment. Trousers, dresses, suits, shirts and bikinis can all be made to measure. Women's ready-to-wear shops often sell good, cheap local copies of the latest European fashions. Tropical sports shirts may also be bought off the peg.

Gems: precious stones such as sapphires and rubies are mined in Thailand, while others are imported at favourable prices from Burma, India, Sri Lanka and other countries. Bangkok claims to be the world's top gem-cutting centre. Seek out a reputable shop and try to avoid unrealistic bargains: fakes are very common.

Handicrafts: with great skill, patience and ingenuity, the artisans of Thailand produce an apparently endless variety of hand-crafted objects. Each region has its specialities.

Ivory: Chinese-style elephant sculptures, Mandarin figurines, as well as incredible one-piece globe-within-globe follies.

Jewellery: Thai designers tend towards traditional styles, but originals can be ordered. Pick carefully where you shop; the establishments which cater to tour buses often pay the travel agency a 20 percent kick-back on what you spend. Thai costume jewellery can be cheap.

Kites: fighting models, neatly folded, make an original gift.

Lacquerware: pretty gold and black boxes in the shape of fantasy animals.

Mobiles: cheerful hanging ensembles; bells made of shell.

Whether originally intended to cool the face or for coy ladies to hide behind, colourful fans are still sold throughout Thailand.

In Chiang Mai and the village of Bor Sang, intricate touches are added to colourful umbrellas.

Nielloware: black metal alloy inlaid on silver for trinkets.

Old books: look for old Burmese manuscripts – on parchment, illuminated, and bound in leather.

Pottery: a typical Thai variety – *benjarong* ware – has a five-coloured design on a background of grey, white or black. Also, patterned porcelain jars, plates, pots, even spitoons.

Rattan goods: lightweight furniture; peasant hats.

Seashells: notable bargains at Thai beach resorts, in shops or from itinerant vendors.

Tape cassettes: both Thai and international pop and classical music at bargain prices, mostly 'pirate tapes', but good value.

Thai silk and fabrics: happy silkworms keep thousands of nimble weavers busy, hand and foot, in producing the famous, colourful Thai fabrics. Ranging from lightweight blouses to heavy bedspreads, the long-lasting fibres live up to their worldwide reputation. Durable Thai cotton, most of which is factory-made, goes into ready-to-wear clothing, towels, some toys and tablecloths. Keep an eye open for brightly coloured padded jackets.

Umbrellas: all around Chiang Mai, locals make hand-painted parasols, large and small – to your own design, if you wish.

Woodcarvings: figurines, teak furniture, salad bowls and a variety of other knick-knacks.

Xylophones: the Thai versions, known as *ranad ek* and *ranad thum* (treble and alto respectively), have wooden bars on a boat-shaped soundbox.

Zoological curiosities: moths and butterflies with Latin captions; stuffed cobras poised to strike; stuffed mongooses as antidote.

Entertainment

Mention Bangkok to anybody and the chances are they'll ask you about the city's nightlife. Indeed, from nightclubs to go-go bars, Thailand hums with excitement – even early birds will not be able to miss it.

There are also a few quieter things to do for family entertainment. Nightclubs, mostly in the major hotels, feature live bands, floor shows and dancing. Bangkok offers discos, as well as more intimate places where combo or piano music is played, plus bars and pubs for friendly conversation.

Various nightclub-style restaurants specialize in traditional Thai food and music; the floor show consists of performances by Thai dancers, regional folklore or both.

Otherwise, cultural possibilities suitable for foreign visitors are quite limited. Visiting musicians sometimes perform, as do local theatre groups. Due to a stiff tax on imported films, very few foreign imports are shown. This is supposed to encourage the Thai film industry, **105** which still produces a constant stream of second-rate movies. Some bars, clubs, hotels, and even a few associations, fill the gap by showing imported films on a semi-private basis. You might also want to check the listings in the local English-language newspapers.

The Go-Go Scene

In just Bangkok alone you can choose from several hundred nightclubs and go-go bars, and throughout the country several thousand more. These, along with the thousands of escorts and dancers who work in them, cater to every taste, from easy conversation to the unabashed hedonism of the girlie bars and the mind-boggling acrobatics of the upstairs bars.

Although they are obviously aimed at single, heterosexual males, women are usualy welcome to come in for a drink and a look. Also, gay bars are increasingly run in the same areas, particularly in Bangkok and Chiang Mai.

In Patpong – usually seen as **106** the best-known red-light area

of the lot (more people visit it every year than the Grand Palace) – there are even markets, pizza shops and Thai boxing displays for entertainment.

Before you go, remember a few words of warning. Upstairs bars are frequently a front for live sex shows and may try to charge vast amounts of money. Wise people always check the price before entering a bar; if there is trouble, simply pay the bill and get in touch with the tourist police. Pimps, including many taxi drivers, are good at making enticing suggestions which, were you to take them up, would usually be more expensive than you would anticipate. Touts who hang around outside hotels and bars know where to find live sex shows and other pornographic diversions. However, strictly speaking these are illegal and could be raided by the police.

Women, too, are not always what they seem – transvestites might well give clients more than they bargained for. AIDS and other venereal diseases are also rife (just count the number of VD clinics).

Provincial nightlife is often calmer than that in the capital, though many towns have night-clubs with hostesses for hire, massage parlours and the like. Pattaya has a comprehensive nightlife comparing favourably with Bangkok's. Down in the far south, Hat Yai outdoes all other provincial towns with a highly concentrated entertainment zone that attracts crowds of tourists from across the border in Malaysia.

Festivals and Holidays

The list below details only a few of the principal events that have made Thailand renowned as one of the Far East's most colourful nations. Check dates before you leave, however, as many depend on the position of the sun or the moon.

February: flower carnival in Chiang Mai. Floats; parades.

April: the *Songkran* or Water Festival is most uninhibitedly celebrated in Chiang Mai, but is also fun in Bangkok.

May: the timing of the Royal Ploughing Ceremony is determined by the king's Brahmin astrologers, and comes just before the rainy season. The king presides over the ceremonies at Pramane Ground, Bangkok.

May: *Boon Fai* (rocket) festival. Drums, dances, fireworks. Mostly in the northeast.

July: *Asanha Puja*. Candlelit processions by full moon at every temple in Thailand.

October-November: the end of the rainy season and Buddhist Lent comes with *Kathin*; processions bear gifts of robes and utensils to the monks.

November: *Loi Krathong*, at the full moon; candles and incense are floated down canals on banana-leaf boats, notably in Bangkok and Chiang Mai. Also, the elephant Round-up in Surin in the north east, when TAT and provincial authorities move hundreds of elephants.

Eating Out

Good food in Thailand is as ubiquitous as beaches – and often quite a lot hotter besides. If you don't like chillies, however, don't give up on the food. *Mai phet* (not hot), stressed at the time you order, can bring a delicious selection of cooler, more subtle flavours, that may include any taste ranging from the sweetness of coconut milk to the pungency of fresh herbs, lemon grass, garlic or nutmeg and the saltiness of fermented fish. Added to that are tropical fruits such as fresh pineapple, a little sugar, a pinch of coriander – and, of course, a lashing of culinary inspiration.

Every region boasts its own specialities. Up in the north, a local sausage known as *naem* is popular, while the northeast is famed for its sticky or glutinous rice (*khao nia*), normally served as an accompaniment to barbecued meat (generally buffalo), as well as *som tam*, a hot salad that combines shredded green papaya with dried shrimps or curried crab claws, lemon juice, garlic, fish sauce and chillies.

The south produces numerous dishes that have been influenced by the Muslim style of cooking of the Malays and, of course, all kinds of seafood dishes, including crab, squid, shark, freshly cooked lobsters and mussels.

Don't worry if you have a sweet tooth – you're not likely to go hungry at all. Many Thai sweets are based on rice flour, coconut milk, palm sugar and sticky rice, and just about all of them are delicious.

What to Eat

If you are a newcomer to Thai food, start off with something mild (*mai phet*) and then work up to pig's intestines soup or chillied serpents' heads! Also a good start are curries (*kaeng pet*) – particularly those with a coconut cream base, which are less piquant than European or Indian varieties – and there is never any shortage of wonderful fresh fish.

When eating chillies, take a local tip and have plenty of

steamed rice, which helps to soothe the stomach and will smother the fire. Nothing else is as effective, and cold drinks are certainly one of the worst antidotes possible.

Appetizers: *paw pia tod* is a Thai spring roll – a crisp pancake which encloses a sweet-and-sour feast of bean sprouts, pork and crabmeat.

Gai hor bai toey consists of chunks of chicken fried with sesame oil, soya sauce, oyster sauce, herbs and just a drop of whisky, all in a leaf wrapper.

Soup: *tom yam* is a hot-sour soup, made with either pork,

The desire to please – namchai – is the hallmark of Thailand's top hotels, which rank amongst the best in the world.

shrimp, beef, chicken or fish, that must be accompanied by plenty of steamed rice to soak up the excess chilli heat. Note the fanciful selection of herbs and leaves which are left floating in the big bowl.

Gaeng jeud is a less pungent soup made from chicken, pork and shrimp cooked with Chinese-style vegetables and Thai herbs and spices.

Rice and noodles: *kao pad* is fried rice with whatever bits of meat come to hand.

Mee grob is crispy fried rice noodles with pork, egg, bean sprouts, shrimp and a sweet-and-sour flavour.

Bah mee nam is a rich broth of thin noodles, pork or chicken chunks, mixed with herbs, bean sprouts and subtle spices. This is a filling soup, more like a main dish.

Seafood: *hor mok pla* is a fish curry with vegetables and coconut milk, served wrapped in banana leaves.

Pla preow wan is fried fish covered in a thick sweet-and-sour sauce.

110

Gung tod – or crispy fried prawns – usually comes with a choice of sauces.

Meat: *gaeng mud-sa-man* is a beef curry which is less spicy than most and has an overtone of peanuts.

Kao nah gai is sliced chicken with spring onion, bamboo shoots and steamed rice.

Sa lad neua san translates as roast beef salad and also contains vegetables, chillies, garlic and perhaps mint.

Sweets: *salim* is a refreshing sweet of sugared noodles with coconut milk and crushed ice.

Ice-cream, pronounced *eye-cream*, sometimes comes in original and natural flavours. A local variation of a sundae, for instance, is coconut ice-cream sprinkled with peanuts and kernels of corn.

Fruit: *somo*, meaning pomelo, is something akin to a tropical cousin of the grapefruit and is served divided into sections.

Sap-pa-rot, pineapple, is a familiar fruit but twice as tasty on its home ground.

More exotic local fruits are rarely on restaurant menus, but can be discovered at markets and on street stalls. Just point if you don't know the name.

Ngor (rambutan) looks like an overdeveloped hairy strawberry; the fruit is inside.

Lamut, a light-brown fruit that has to be peeled, is syrupy sweet, with a taste reminiscent of fresh figs.

Durian, that monster with spiky thorns, contains bits of custard-like fruit around egg-shaped piths; its smell is often thought to be more oppressive than a rubbish tip.

Try delicious local oranges, bananas, mangoes, papayas ... almost every fruit imaginable, except apples and pears, which don't grow here and are imported and expensive.

Curiosities

There is no need to hold back on quantity or to restrict yourself to one dish, for Thais will generally order a selection and share them as a group.

Thai restaurants often welcome customers with cold, and even sometimes frozen, hand-towels, as a relief from the tropical world outside. Many restaurants have also taken to issuing disposable mini-towels in small plastic packets; the explosions you hear all about you are the Thais smacking the air-tight packs to open them.

Don't expect to find knives on Thai tables – a spoon is used instead. Salt and pepper cellars will also be absent – the piquancy of the food is such that it is unlikely you'll need them. A few new sauces may be offered, however.

Nam prik, 'pepper water', is a much prized concoction of pounded red chillies, shrimp paste, black pepper, garlic and onions, mixed with tamarind, lemon juice, ginger, and fish in an early state of fermentation.

If you do find the food undersalted, add a little *nam pla*, a caramel-coloured fish sauce with tiny chilli segments in it. Small bowls of roasted chillies from the famous *prik kee noo* ('mouse-shit pepper') to the potent *prik chii faa* are also served on the side – for diners of a more robust constitution. **111**

When in Asia ...

For a change of both taste and scenery, try one of the various Asian restaurants that serve a spectrum of different cuisines – almost all of them at bargain prices. By far the most common is Chinese food. In Bangkok you can sample the most important regional schools of Chinese cooking – Szechuan Canton, Shanghai and Peking – as well as the less familiar food of the Hakka, Chiu Chow and Hunan people.

Restaurants specializing in food from neighbouring Cambodia, Malaysia, Burma, and Laos are not easy to find, but more distant and better-known cuisines – like Japanese and Korean – are well represented, having become more popular alongside the tourist trade.

For quite different reasons, including the flow of refugees, Vietnamese restaurants have become noticeably more widespread. The significant population of Thais of Indian descent or Muslim religion accounts for the availability of curries and associated foods.

Western cuisine

Most hotels serve an approximation of European food. For greater authenticity, try out the various nationality restaurants, many in Bangkok owned by foreign residents. Among the possibilities are French, American, German, Hungarian, Italian, Scandinavian, British and Swiss cooking.

Drinks

Iced water is frequently served at the start of a meal. It's almost bound to be safe to drink in any decent restaurant, but if in doubt, ask for a bottle of water and skip the ice. Thais usually drink water or cold tea (*cha jin yen*) throughout their meal, along with whisky with dinner. You can drink anything you please and the Thais will not be surprised: iced coffee or iced tea, soft drinks, milk, fruit juice, beer or lemonade. Thai lemonade is normally salted to fight dehydration in the hot climate: you may not appreciate the taste, but it helps to avoid covering all your food in salt.

All wines are disastrously expensive in Thailand, costing several times the price in their country of origin. Even in a modest restaurant, an undistinguished wine could cost more than the whole dinner.

Thailand does produce good beer, though, and brand names to try are Singha, Kloster and Amarit – all are stronger than you expect or think.

Thai whisky, on the other hand, is weaker and cheaper than you'd think (Mekhong is the best-known brand), though this, too, can result in frighteningly bad hangovers.

F ish in a basket – the average Thai eats more than 11 kilos of seafood each year.

To Help You Order ...

Could we have a table ...?	ขอโต๊ะ...ได้ไหม?	*kor toh ...dai mai?*
I'd like a/an/some ...	ผม(ดิฉัน)อยากได้...	*Chan yak cha ...*
beer	เบียร์	*beer*
bread	ขนมปัง	*kha-nome-pung*
coffee	กาแฟ	*kafae*
meat	เนื้อ	*neua*
menu	รายการอาหาร	*raigarn arharn*
milk	นม	*nom*
rice	ข้าว	*kao*
salt	เกลือ	*keua*
soup	ซุป	*soop*
sugar	น้ำตาล	*nam thal*
tea	ชา	*cha*
water	น้ำ	*nam*

... and Read the Menu

เนื้อวัว	*neua*	beef
ไก่	*gai*	chicken
แกง	*gaeng*	curry
ไข่	*khai*	egg
ปลา	*pla*	fish
ก๋วยเตี๋ยว	*kwaytio*	noodles
เนื้อหมู	*moo*	pork
กุ้ง	*gung*	shrimp
114 แตงโม	*taeng-mo*	watermelon

BLUEPRINT
for a
Perfect Trip

An A–Z Summary of Practical Information

A

ACCOMMODATION (See also CAMPING on p.117, YOUTH HOSTELS on p.139 and RECOMMENDED HOTELS on pp.66-73)

The balance between supply and demand in Bangkok and the major tourist destinations varies enormously, but advance reservations for hotel rooms are always a good idea. Bangkok has 35,000 rooms considered suitable for foreign tourists; budget travellers will find many no-frills, native-style hotels as well. Of the former, even the cheapest are completely air-conditioned, and many have swimming pools and other comforts. International-standard hotels are also found in the beach resorts and regional capitals such as Chiang Mai and Hat Yai.

In smaller towns, facilities may be fairly basic – but so are prices.

Do you have a (double) room? **Mee hong (kuu) mai?**

AIRPORTS

Don Muang international airport (tel. 535 1254–departures; 535 1301 arrivals; 535 1111 directory assistance), 30km (18 miles) north of Bangkok, is Thailand's principal gateway, and the arrival and departure terminals are up to the highest international standards, with a selection of duty-free shops. Immigration and customs clearances are efficient and swift. In the arrival hall, a full range of facilities, including porters, limousine service, hotel desks and a Tourism Authority of Thailand (TAT) information bureau, is available 24 hours a day. Local telephone calls can be made free of charge from call boxes in the arrival and departure halls.

City taxis (without yellow plates) can be taken to the centre, but airport taxis and limousines are better, safer and more likely to have English-speaking drivers. Cheaper (for lone-travellers) air-conditioned mini buses also pick up at the terminal, but are much slower alternatives. From the airport to Bangkok's hotels takes between 45 minutes and 3 hours, depending on the traffic.

Those heading for Pattaya can take an air-conditioned coach there directly from the airport (about a three-hour trip).

Internal flights. Although buses and trains are usually comfortable, the fast (but more expensive) way to reach the far north or south is by air. Domestic airlines run a comprehensive service of jet and turbo-prop flights to all parts of the country, including Chiang Mai in the north and Ko Samui, Phuket and Hat Yai in the south.

B

BICYCLE and MOPED HIRE
Although not advisable in the horror of Bangkok traffic, bikes can be rented at several hotels and guesthouses. At beach resorts such as Pattaya, Ko Samui and Phuket, bikes and mopeds can be hired through your hotel reception or travel counter. Distant beaches and Chiang Mai lend themselves to exploration by bike or moped.

BOAT TRIPS (See also GUIDES AND TOURS on p.124)
Guided boat tours are a pleasant, if expensive, way to see Bangkok's river and canals. For cheap, do-it-yourself sightseeing, take the river-bus (*baht* boat) – only a few baht for an hour's trip up or down the mighty Chao Phya. For the canals, private long-tailed boats (*hang yao*) may be rented from outside the Oriental Hotel or from river stops at the Grand Palace (Tha Chang) and Wat Po (Tha Thien).

C

CAMPING
Several national parks offer camping facilities, as do a number of the islands. Camping is not recommended outside in the wilds, as rob-beries and hold-ups are not uncommon.

CAR HIRE (See also DRIVING on p.120)

To rent a car you must be over 21 and hold an international driving licence. You may be asked for a deposit equal to the estimated final cost, though some companies may waive this for credit-card holders.

Insurance is usually offered on a daily basis at extra cost.

CHILDREN'S THAILAND

Children take to Thailand like ducks to water. The main problem is the heat. Bring a lot of sun cream, and ask doctors about vaccinations and other requirements. Although there is lots to keep children amused, reaching attractions in Bangkok can involve a 2-hour drive.

CLIMATE

Thailand enjoys its best weather just when the northern temperate zone is suffering the worst of winter. November to February are the favoured months in Bangkok, ironically known as the 'cool season', when the temperature dips a bit below the usual debilitating extreme and, more important, the humidity is lower. Rain is quite rare.

The following chart for Bangkok gives the average maximum and minimum daily temperatures and number of rainy days per month:

		J	F	M	A	M	J	J	A	S	O	N	D
average daily	°F	89	91	93	95	93	91	90	90	89	88	87	87
maximum	°C	32	33	34	35	34	33	32	32	32	31	31	31
average daily	°F	68	72	75	77	77	76	76	76	76	75	72	68
minimum	°C	20	22	24	25	25	25	24	24	24	24	22	20
rainy days		2	2	4	5	14	16	19	21	23	17	7	1

Although temperatures of 36-38°C (around 100°F) are common in the hot season, widespread use of air-conditioning relieves discomfort. The rainy season (monsoon) lasts from about June to October. It rains mostly in the afternoon or evening, cooling and refreshing the tropical air, and inundating the streets.

CLOTHING

Pack for the tropics: the more cotton the better. A light sweater might come in handy if you are planning a trip to the hills; the only other place you may feel cold is in a strongly air-conditioned restaurant.

Immodesty should be avoided: adults should not wear shorts when visiting temples, and women with plunging necklines will receive plenty of stares, not all admiring. The Thais are strict about covering up, except on the beach, but are quite casual as regards dressing up – even the Grand Palace no longer requires jackets and ties. Almost all restaurants and nightclubs share the same informal approach.

COMPLAINTS (See also POLICE on p.131)

If you have a dispute with a hotel, merchant or any organization or person in Thailand, it is important not to lose your temper. If your complaint has no effect after you have tried approaching the person or establishment concerned directly, consult the Tourism Authority of Thailand. In serious cases, the tourist police can often be of assistance in resolving the problem.

CRIME (See also EMERGENCIES on p.122)

Beware of pickpockets in crowded marketplaces. Purse-snatchers are now motorized in Bangkok, fleeing on a motorbike almost before the victim realizes what's happened. Don't tempt bandits by flaunting jewels or ostentatious clothes, and never leave irreplaceable items in your hotel room; use the safe-deposit box, but get an official receipt.

At seaside resorts, never leave any valuables on the beach when you go swimming. At Phuket, the authorities advise tourists to avoid isolated beaches, where they might be accosted by itinerant robbers.

CUSTOMS and ENTRY FORMALITIES
(See also MEDICAL CARE on pp.126-127)

Citizens of most countries need tourist visas to stay more than 30 days in Thailand. For the latest regulations, check with your travel agent or the Thai consulate in your own country. So-called undesirable tourists – meaning presumed 'hippies' – may be refused entry, or required to prove financial responsibility. Any visitor may be asked to prove his or her solvency by producing the equivalent of Bt10,000 (per person) or Bt20,000 (per family) upon arrival (in currency, traveller's cheques or credit cards).

Duty Free. On entering Thailand, you may take in 200 cigarettes *or* 250 cigars *or* 250g tobacco, plus one litre of *either* spirits *or* wine.

Currency restrictions. There is no restriction on the import of foreign currency, but amounts over the equivalent of 10,000 US dollars must be declared. On leaving the country, you may take out up to 10,000 US dollars or the equivalent in foreign currency (more if declared on arrival). Gold jewellery and video cameras must also be declared when you arrive.

When leaving Thailand, note that the export of any images of Buddha or other deities is prohibited. It is also prohibited to export antiquities without special permission from the Fine Arts Department. Some shops will be able to handle this for you. Alternatively, you can contact the office directly:

National Museum, Fine Arts Department, 4 Na Phratatu Road, Bangkok; tel. 226 1661.

D

DRIVING

As in many Asian countries, traffic in Thailand is supposed to keep to the left. Due to chronic traffic jams, driving conditions in the Bangkok metropolis are appalling; peak traffic persists almost all day with only brief periods of respite. On the main highways out of town, free-spirited drivers make up their own rules as they go along, using whatever part of the road they feel they need, even if it means running another car into a ditch. As you discover the local driving customs, you won't need reminding to stay extremely alert. Watch out, too, for buses in one-way streets going in the opposite direction to the traffic. The official speed limit is 40kmh (25mph) in towns, **120** 80kmh (50mph) on highways.

Fuel and oil. Readily available in both regular and super.

Breakdowns. Telephone the rental firm from which you hired the car to come and rescue you. In an emergency dial the Highway Police Patrol Centre; tel. 193.

Parking. Car parks and metered parking are found on some streets.

Distance

Fluid measures

Road signs. Many Thai road signs are standard international pictographs. Speed limits are always posted in arabic numerals.

Accident	**u bat hed**
Collision	**rod chon**
Flat tyre	**yang bean**
Help!	**chuey duey!**
Police!	**tam ruat!**

DRUGS

Most of the big narcotics arrests in Thailand involve people caught trying to smuggle drugs out for sale abroad. Possession of heroin or its variants for trade and distribution is punishable by five years to life imprisonment (foreigners), death sentence (Thais) and a fine of up to half a million baht. Possessing, trading or smoking of marijuana or related substances is punishable by as much as six months in prison. Ignorance of Thai law is not a mitigating factor in drug cases. **121**

ELECTRIC CURRENT

The standard current in Thailand is 220-volt, 50-cycle AC; most hotel rooms have a point for shavers; some have 110-volt sockets too.

EMBASSIES and CONSULATES

For a complete list of embassies and consulates see the yellow pages of the Bangkok telephone directory under 'Embassies, Consulates & Legations'. For Thai visa problems, consult the Tourism Authority of Thailand or the government Immigration Division; tel. 286 9065.

Australia: 37 Sathon Tai Road; tel. 212 5853/4; 8am–12.30pm and 1.45–4pm Monday to Friday.

Canada: Boonmitr Building, 11th & 12th floors, 138 Silom Road; tel. 237 4126; visa section 9.30am–12pm Monday to Friday; other sections 7.30am–12.15pm and 1–4.15pm.

Eire: United Flour Mills Building, 11th floor, 105 Rajawongse Road; tel. 223 0876, 223-0470/9; 9am–2pm Monday to Friday.

Japan: 1674 New Photohaburi Road; tel. 252 6151/9.

New Zealand: 93 Witthayu Road; tel. 251 8165; 8am–12pm and 1–4pm Monday to Friday.

United Kingdom: 1031 Ploenchit Road; tel. 253 0191/9; 8am-12am, 1.30–4pm Monday to Thursday, 8am–1pm Friday.

USA: 95 Witthayu Road; tel. 252 5170/9; 7.30am–12pm and 1–4.30pm Monday to Friday.

EMERGENCIES

The main hospitals treat urgent medical problems 24 hours a day; below are some useful telephone numbers:

Bangkok General Hospital	318 0066
Bangkok Mission (Adventist) Hospital	281 1442

| Primmitr Hospital | 259 0373/8 |
| Police Hospital, Rajdamri Road | 252 8111 |

Provincial towns also have fully equipped hospitals.

The following numbers may also be useful in an emergency:

Tourist Assistance Centre (Bangkok)	282 8189, 281 5051
Highway Police Patrol Centre	193
Fire	199 or Bangkok 246 0199
Ambulance	252 2171/5
All-purpose emergency number	**191**

ETIQUETTE

Ignorance of Thai sensibilities can cause much embarrassment. The monarchy is greatly revered, so the slightest indication of disrespect, even accidental, could have serious consequences. This even applies to money bearing the king's likeness.

Religion plays a most important part in the life of the Thais. When you visit a temple, dress soberly – no shorts or revealing blouses. Wear shoes, but you must remove them before entering the chapel. Never show disrespect to a religious object or to Buddhist monks and nuns (don't offer money to a monk, but you can offer a cigarette). Women are not allowed in certain temples nor should they touch monks or novices or hand anything directly to them.

Note that since the head is considered sacred, you must not touch anyone there. Don't point your feet towards another person's body (remember this especially in temples, where you'll see worshippers' feet tucked behind them), and don't use them to open a door. Don't lose your temper or display strong emotion (including boisterous thanks). Finally, in spite of Bangkok's reputation, public displays of affection between the sexes are frowned upon.

Remember, Thailand may be known as the 'Land of Smiles', but a smile can just as easily conceal disapproval as imply acceptance. **123**

GETTING TO THAILAND

Because of the complexity and variety of fares available, you should ask the advice of an informed travel agent well before departure.

BY AIR

Scheduled flights. Bangkok's Don Muang international airport (see AIRPORTS on p.116) is the principal gateway to Thailand and a major airport of entry to the Far East. Regular services arrive from Europe, America, Canada, Australia and Asia. The flight from London takes roughly 14 hours, from New York 24 hours, from Sydney 13 hours.

Charter flights and package tours. *From the UK and Eire*: a wide range of package tours to Thailand, or tours featuring Thailand as part of a package, are available. Among the most popular is the 'fly-cruise': you fly to Bangkok or Singapore, then cruise from there to Bali, Jakarta and other Far Eastern ports. *From North America*: Several tour operators offer Group Inclusive Tour (GIT) programmes that feature Bangkok along with other exotic ports of call in the Far East. From 15 to 30 days in length, these tours include air transport between scheduled cities, transfers to and from hotels, hotel accommodation, some sightseeing and the services of an English-speaking guide, some or all meals, as well as tips and service charges. These GITs may be extended to include a stop-over in Hawaii.

BY ROAD

Private car travel to Thailand is almost impossible, as the Burmese border is closed. Cars can be driven in from Malaysia and Singapore.

BY RAIL

From Singapore, trains travel through Malaysia to Bangkok, including the new luxury service run by the world-famous *Venice-Simplon Orient Express*, known as the *Eastern and Oriental Express*.

GUIDES and TOURS

The enterprising Bangkok travel trade has devised scores of excursions for tourists, from the floating market boat trip to archaeological outings. Nine pages of agencies are listed in the classified telephone directory under 'Travel Bureaux'. For interpreters, see the entry 'Translators and Interpreters' in the yellow pages. Avoid unauthorized guides who greet you on the street and offer to show you Bangkok (see Touts on p.136).

HELPLINES

Disabled travellers. Although lift services are available in all big hotels, and wheelchairs can be found at local airports, facilities for disabled travellers are few and far between. For further information contact the Association for the Disabled in Bangkok, tel. 463 5929.

Women travelling alone. Precautions apply as for any country or city. Main tourist areas are safe, and you shouldn't stray off these on your own at night. On arrival to any main city in Thailand, go to the Tourist Assistance Centre, who will be able to advise and help you.

Gay & Lesbian. Thailand does not openly accept homosexuality, though it does tolerate it. However, there is no gay switchboard, and you are pretty much left to your own devices.

LANGUAGE (See also Useful Expressions on pp.139-140)

Although English is widely used in hotels and shops – it's the best-known Western language in Thailand – try to express some simple phrases in Thai. The Thai language spoken in Bangkok is understood everywhere in the country, though there are many dialects and sub-dialects. In addition, several other languages are widely used, such as Lao in the northeast, Malay in the south, and the Teochiu dialect of Chinese in many different areas. Like Chinese, Thai uses intonation to distinguish between otherwise identical words, which makes it a difficult language for foreigners. Each syllable can have up to five different meanings depending on how it is pronounced; there are 44 **125** consonants plus dozens of vowels, compounds and tone marks. If all this doesn't discourage you, consider Rachasap, a special language used only when speaking to or about Thai royalty!

Try to imitate a Thai to learn how to intone these useful words; your efforts will be appreciated by everyone you meet. You will find a list of useful expressions on the cover of this guide.

LAUNDRY and DRY CLEANING

Many hotels will arrange your laundry for you, returning it within 24 hours and even within four hours at premium rates. Dry cleaning takes two days unless 'express service' is specified, when it takes half the time but costs 50 percent extra. Laundries and dry-cleaners are listed under 'Laundries' in the classified telephone directory. There are some semi-self-service laundrettes in Thailand.

LOST PROPERTY

If you lose something, check with your hotel receptionist, then report the loss to the nearest police station or, in Bangkok, to the Tourist Assistance Centre (see TOURIST INFORMATION OFFICES on p.135).

MAPS

The Tourism Authority of Thailand issues free bus and tourist maps showing the principal attractions of Bangkok. These aren't always adequate though, and it is better to buy one of the commercially produced maps of Bangkok and Thailand that are sold at hotels and bookshops. Interesting specialized maps of the waterways and markets of Bangkok are also available.

MEDICAL CARE

Don't let the heat get you down. If you are not used to the tropics, respect the midday sun; it can broil you in an hour. To avoid dehydration, have plenty of salt on your breakfast eggs (the Thais put salt in their lemonade). Spare your digestive system by experimenting gradually until you're more accustomed to the spicy Thai cuisine. Wear light, airy clothing and a hat in the sun, and don't go anywhere barefoot (because of snakes).

Check with your doctor before leaving home for recommendations on **malaria** prevention. While Bangkok and other principal towns are malaria-free, the disease can be found in some parts of Thailand. Hotels often have doctors on call; alternatively, look one up in the classified (yellow) pages of the telephone directory under 'Physicians and Surgeons'.

Bangkok has efficient, modern hospitals staffed by well-qualified personnel. Since health care can be expensive, make sure you have arranged an adequate insurance policy covering illness or accident on holiday before you go.

Chemists' shops are open from about 9am-9pm, and later in some areas. Most foreign drugs are available, though it's wise to check the expiry date on the package. Many drugs that are normally available by prescription only can be bought over the counter. If you do decide to be your own doctor, it's worth asking for a printed advice note on the side effects of whatever drugs you buy.

I need a doctor.	**pom/chan tong karn maw.**
I need a dentist.	**pom/chan tong kan maw fang.**

Vaccinations. Visitors arriving in Thailand should have certificates proving the validity of their cholera, yellow fever and smallpox vaccinations if they are coming from infected areas. The risk of malaria exists in rural areas all over the country. Vaccinations against both cholera and typhoid are particularly recommended. Check with your doctor well before departure for the latest information and advice.

MONEY MATTERS

The unit of currency in Thailand is the baht (abbreviated Bt or B), divided into 100 satang. Banknotes come in denominations of 10, 20, 50, 100, 500 and 1,000 baht. Coins are 25 and 50 satang, 1, 5 and 10 baht. Note that 1-baht coins are found in two different sizes (it's only the small one that can be used in most street telephones). The 5-baht coin is also available in two sizes, but can be distinguished from the large 1-baht coin by the copper streak on the edge.

A number of minibuses have now been converted into motorized currency-exchange units. They circulate through the streets of central Bangkok, Pattaya, Phuket and Chiang Mai.

Banks and exchange facilities. Normally the exchange rate at banks is the most favourable. After the banks are closed you can change money at your hotel, at exchange booths or at shops displaying a sign in English saying 'money-changer'.

Banks and money-changers in tourist towns will accept virtually any currency. There is no black market in pounds or dollars, and carrying them with you can constitute a security risk. The best way is to take traveller's cheques or use credit cards.

Credit cards. Major hotels, restaurants and shops are accustomed to the well-known international charge cards. One or two major cards can be used in cash-withdrawal machines, but as the instructions are sometimes in Thai script, it can be easier to go inside, where you will need your passport for identification.

Prices. See also PLANNING YOUR BUDGET on p.129. Heavier taxes on hotels, restaurants and entertainment make Thailand less of a tourist bargain than in the recent past, and imported goods are always expensive. Still, transport is cheap, especially buses.

Thai and Chinese food can be a great bargain, though foreign ingredients, cooking styles and decor raise the price considerably. The worst blow in restaurants is the price of wine, but Thai beer and even undistinguished local whisky are inexpensive.

Bargaining. Many foreigners feel uncomfortable with it, but bargaining over prices is customary in several areas of Thai life. For instance, the prices in almost all taxis (except those clearly labelled meter taxis) are negotiated in advance. More protracted bargaining takes place when shopping for souvenirs and in other aspects of commerce; even hotels sometimes have flexible rates. The squeamish can either accept the first price mentioned (which would astound a market trader) or take a fixed-price hotel taxi to one of the big department stores, where the price tags mean business.

PLANNING YOUR BUDGET

To give an idea of what to expect, here are some average prices in Thai baht (Bt). They are only approximate, as inflation takes its toll.

Airport. Limousine service to city-centre: from international terminal Bt350; from domestic terminal Bt300 (taxi minimally less). Airport departure tax: international flights Bt200, domestic flights Bt20.

Boats. Long-tailed boats and motorized river boats around Bt300 per hour (negotiable); private two-hour canal cruise Bt500 per boat.

Buses. City buses Bt2.5-3.5, air-conditioned buses Bt6-16 within city boundary. Air-conditioned coach Bangkok–Pattaya (one way) Bt60 (private operators, pick-up from major hotels). Air-conditioned coach Bangkok–Phuket (one way) Bt600 (private operators).

Car hire (international company). Toyota Corolla 1300/Nissan Sunny 1200 Bt1,700 per day; Bt10,000 per week, unlimited mileage.

Entertainment. Nightclub entry, two drinks and a floor show Bt200.

Guided tours. Floating market morning tour Bt300. All-day river excursion to Ayutthaya (with lunch) Bt900.

Hairdressers (in top hotels; elsewhere prices considerably lower). Women's haircut Bt500, shampoo and set Bt200. Man's haircut Bt400, shave Bt100, shampoo Bt150-200.

Hotels (air-conditioned double room with bath). Budget Bt500-1,000, Tourist Bt1,000-2,000, First class Bt2,500-4,000. Luxury Bt4,000 and up. Add 10 percent service charge and 11 percent taxes. These rates are for peak months (December–March), and are considerably less at other times.

Meals and drinks. Hotel breakfast Bt150-300, lunch Bt300, dinner Bt500, including 10 per cent service charge and 7 per cent taxes. Beer (local) Bt50, wine (imported) at least Bt350 per bottle.

Taxis. Bt35-80 in central Bangkok (hotel taxis cost twice as much).

Trains. Bangkok–Chiang Mai: first class, one way Bt837, return Bt1,428; second class, one way Bt315, couchette Bt100 extra. Bangkok–Hat Yai: second-class couchette (one way) Bt500.

NEWSPAPERS and MAGAZINES

Bangkok has four English language dailies, *Bangkok Post*, *The Nation*, *Thailand Times* and *Business Day* to complement its big range of Thai and Chinese papers. Newspapers from elsewhere in Asia and Europe are sold in the major hotels and bookshops. English-language magazines and paperback books are also available.

OPENING HOURS

Banks: 8.30am-3.30pm, Monday to Friday. In seaside tourist areas, most banks operate a foreign-exchange service for tourists until 8pm, seven days a week.

Department stores: around 10am-8.30pm (usually 10pm in Bangkok), often seven days a week. Hours are extended at Christmas, New Year and Chinese New Year.

Government offices: 8.30am-noon and 1-4.30pm, from Monday to Friday.

Museums: around 9am-noon and 1-4.30 pm, every day except Monday and Tuesday.

Post offices: Bangkok's head post office is open 8am-8pm, Monday to Friday and 8am-1pm weekends and holidays.

District post offices 8am-6pm, Monday to Friday and 8am-1 pm weekends and holidays. Telegraph office in General Post Office Building: 24 hours a day, seven days a week.

130 **Small shops**: early morning until 7 or 8pm, often seven days a week.

PHOTOGRAPHY and VIDEO

The golden spires, blue skies, green fields and lush flowers of Thailand cry out to be photographed. Standard brands and sizes of film are easily available. You can have your pictures processed in one hour (express service) or five hours (standard service). Developed film can also be sent home at 'small package' rates. The best camera/film shop in Bangkok is AV Camera on Silom Road.

A special show consisting of classical dancing, sword fighting and Thai boxing is staged for photographers on Thursday and Sunday mornings at the Oriental Hotel. There are many other opportunities for filming these distinctive pageants, but only here are the conditions so perfect.

One word of warning: resist any temptation to take 'trick' pictures of Buddha statues and other religious objects, or even isolated, dilapidated archaeological relics. For instance, never pose anyone touching a statue. Outraged Thais might accuse you of gross disrespect, however unintended. You should check with your guide if you intend to take pictures in temples or other religious places.

Video. Filming in the Grand Palace is restricted, and in some temples an additional charge is made for the use of video cameras.

POLICE

A special force of Thai Tourist Police operates in crucial areas of Bangkok, such as near tourist attractions and major hotels. Over 100 officers, all of them linguists, stand ready to protect or advise foreigners. They wear the beige military-style uniform of ordinary Thai police with 'Tourist Police' shoulder patches.

POST OFFICES (See also OPENING HOURS on p.130)

Branch offices are scattered throughout Bangkok and, for the convenience of visitors, can also be found at Don Muang Airport. Major hotels also provide postal services.

Mail. You can send letters and postcards airmail, which arrive within four days to a week in America or Europe. Almost all the big hotels offer basic mailing services and many newspaper shops sell stamps.

Telegrams. Branch post offices accept telegrams, but for round-the-clock cable and telex service go to the telecommunications department on the ground floor of the General Post Office on New Road.

PUBLIC HOLIDAYS

Since many Thai holidays are fixed to the lunar calendar, the dates vary from year to year. Banks and government offices close on these days, but daily life is not necessarily disrupted. The only notable exception to this is Chinese New Year, which is not a public holiday in Thailand, but a time when most businesses close.

1 January	New Year's Day
6 April	Chakri Day, honouring Rama I
13 April	Songkran Day, water festival
1 May	Labour Day
5 May	Coronation Day
12 August	HM Queen's Birthday
23 October	Chulalongkorn Day, honouring Rama V
5 December	HM King's Birthday and National Day
10 December	Constitution Day
31 December	New Year's Eve

Movable dates

	Chinese New Year (partly observed)
Maka Puja	Commemoration of meeting at which the Buddha preached the doctrines of Buddhism.
Visakha Puja	Commemoration of the first sermon of the Buddha
Khao Phansa	First day of Buddhist Lent

RADIO and TV

TV. Four Bangkok TV channels broadcast in colour and black-and-white. Many programmes are foreign shows, mostly American, which are dubbed into Thai. These days, an increasing number of hotels have cable satellite television.

Radio. Bangkok's English-language radio stations can be found on FM 95.5Mhz, 105Mhz and 107Mhz. These stations offer music interspersed with hourly bulletins. Reception for BBC and Voice of America short-wave programmes is best in the morning or at night.

RELIGION

In Thailand, more than 90 percent of the population are Theravada Buddhists, but Muslim (especially in southern Thailand), Christian, Hindu and other faiths are well represented. For foreign visitors, Protestant and Catholic services in Bangkok are advertised in Saturday's editions of the *Bangkok Post*. A more complete listing can be found under 'Churches' in the classified telephone directory.

TELEPHONES

Public telephones are located in post offices throughout the country and most of them offer a 24-hour international service. Hotels, railway stations, aiports and department stores may also have telephone booths. Most international calls can be dialled direct or made through the operator (dial 100), by placing them through either the telecommunications department or your hotel switchboard. When you dial overseas direct you may have to wait for a dial tone. Most big hotels normally add a hefty surcharge to international calls.

Useful Telephone Numbers

Airport		535 1111
Railway		223 7010
Bus Station	Northern Terminal	272 5233
	Eastern Terminal	391 2504
	Southern Terminal	435 1199
Directory of Assistance		13
Tourism Authority of Thailand		226 0060, 0072, 0085, 0098
Tourist Police		221 6206/10
Immigration Office		286 9231

For lists of hospitals and other emergency services see EMERGENCIES on pp.122-123.

TIME DIFFERENCES

Although Thailand has officially adopted the Western 12-month calendar, the traditonal lunar calendar is used for ceremonies and everyday activities. Major festivals usually fall in a full moon period. Another difference: dates are calculated from the year Buddha was born (543BC). For instance, the year 2523BE (Buddhist Era) in Thailand corresponds to our year 1980.

Thailand time year-round is GMT plus 7 hours. The following chart shows the time in January in some selected cities.

New York	London	**Bangkok**	Sydney
midnight	5am	**noon**	4pm

TIPPING

In simple, native-style restaurants and snack bars tipping is not customary. It is better to tip nothing at all than to leave a 1-baht tip, which is considered an insult. Taxi drivers are not normally tipped. Further guidance is detailed on the next page:

Barber	10%
Hairdresser	10%
Hotel maid, per week	Bt60 (optional)
Lavatory attendant	Bt5
Porter	Bt10
Tourist guide	15% (optional)
Waiter	10%

TOILETS

Try to find a hotel or restaurant. In luxury establishments the toilets may have an attendant, in which case a tip is appropriate. Away from the main centres, you will encounter Eastern-style, hole-in-the-floor-type toilets. In places without running water, you will always find a huge jar of water nearby. Scoop water out for flushing and washing.

Where are the toilets?	**hong nam yu ti nai?**

TOURIST INFORMATION OFFICES

The Tourism Authority of Thailand (TAT) operates an information stand in the arrivals hall of Bangok's Don Muang international airport. You can also obtain leaflets, maps and advice on the main floor of the organization's head office:

Tourism Authority of Thailand, Head Office, Bamrung Muang Road, Bangkok 10100; tel. 226 0075/6, 8.30am to 4.30pm daily.

At the same address you'll find the Tourist Assistance Centre, which can provide help in all situations. Telephone 281 5051, 282 8129 8.30am to 4.30pm daily. Branch offices of TAT at Chiang Mai, Kanchanaburi, Nakhon Ratchasima (Korat), Pattaya, Hat Yai and Phuket have useful regional information and maps. In Chiang Mai the address is: 105/1 Chiang Mai-Lamphun Road; tel. 248 604.

Overseas representatives of the Tourism Authority of Thailand can be found in the following countries:

Australia: 7th floor, Royal Exchange Building, 56 Pitt Street, Sydney NSW 2000; tel. (02) 247 7549/247 7540

United Kingdom: 49 Albemarle Street, London WIX 3FE; tel. (071) 499 7679.

USA: 5 World Trade Center, Suite 3443, New York, NY 10048; tel. (212) 432 0433; fax (212) 912 0920

TOUTS

In Bangkok and, to a lesser extent, in the larger provincial towns of Thailand, tourists are often pestered by touts, black marketeers and pimps. Some are charmingly convincing, others obnoxiously persistent. The best course is to smile and walk away. If you want a *bona fide* guide, ask a travel agency (see GUIDES AND TOURS on pp.124-125). If you need advice about shopping, ask the Tourism Authority of Thailand for their *Official Shopping Guide* booklet.

TRANSPORT

PUBLIC TRANSPORT

Buses. A well-developed network of city buses serves Bangkok. Fares are very low and service is as good as can be reasonably expected in a traffic-jammed metropolis. Though some of the buses are old and cramped, the new air-conditioned models (for a premium fare along special routes) meet high standards. If you plan to cut your expenses by using buses instead of taxis, invest in one of the Bangkok street maps which show the routes. All city buses have route numbers marked in arabic numerals, but destinations are written in Thai. You don't pay as you get on to a city bus; the conductor, jingling a coin box, will come round to sell you a fixed fare ticket.

Intercity coaches range from rickety veterans to comfortable air-conditioned cruisers, and prices vary accordingly. On the heavily travelled routes, like Bangkok to Pattaya, luxury coaches operated by various companies make frequent departures.

Where's the bus stop?　　　　　　**pai rod may yu ti nai?**

Trains. Although the competing air-conditioned buses often travel faster, Thailand's state railway system provides an efficient means of seeing the country. A train is, after all, an adventure, no less so when amongst a crowd of friendly Thai travellers. There are reasonably luxurious air-conditioned first-class cars, comfortable second-class accommodation (including couchettes, which can be reserved), and old-fashioned, wooden third-class cars. Travel agents, hotel desks and the information office at the main (Hualompong) railway station can advise you on schedules and fares. Bangkok's main stations are:

Hualompong on Rama IV Road – for the north and northeast and for express trains to the south.

Makkasan on Nikom Makkasan Road – for the east.

Thon Buri on Bangkok Noi, Rod Fai Road – for the slower trains to the south.

Telephone **223 7010/20** for general information on rail travel.

TAXIS AND SAMLORS

Taxis. In Bangkok you don't have to whistle for a taxi – just look at one and the driver will jam on the brakes. Taxis are so plentiful that they can be a nuisance, and drivers congregate near hotels and cruise alongside strolling foreigners to solicit business.

Until recently, although virtually all Bangkok taxis had meters, they almost never used them. These days a new, smarter breed of taxi has emerged with a big sign saying 'TAXI-METER'. If you cannot find one of these and opt for an older model, remember that you must haggle over the fare before getting into the cab. Once agreed, the price is a matter of honour; no tip is expected. To make things easier, ask your hotel receptionist to write down your destination in Thai so you can show it to the driver, since foreigners' pronunciation of street or place names is rarely understood. The hotel receptionist should also be able to advise you what the appropriate fare will be. This depends on the distance and the amount of traffic.

If you can't stand the haggling and the language problem, you can take an air-conditioned hotel taxi. The fares are set, and are usually at least twice what a public taxi would cost, but they have the advantage that drivers very often know some English.

Even some of the larger provincial towns have no conventional taxis at all. You can take a *samlor* or, for longer trips, hail an empty minibus. In either case, be sure you agree on the fare in advance.

Samlors/Tuk-Tuks. Useful and adventurous for short trips, these noisy little vehicles nip in and out of Bangkok's traffic. *Samlors* cost a few baht less than four-wheeled taxis and should always be subject to negotiation before you sit down.

WATER
Don't drink the tap water in Thailand. Most hotels place a bottle or flask of purified water in every room. Responsible restaurants serve bottled water and pure ice, but be cautious about the ice in drinks at roadside stands. To be on the safe side in questionable situations, insist on bottled water or soft drinks and beer without ice.

a bottle of drinking water   **nam yen nung khuad**

WEIGHTS and MEASURES
Thailand adopted the metric system more than 50 years ago, but a few traditional measures still exist. The one most frequently seen is the *rai*: 1 *rai* = 0.4 acres (0.16ha).
For fluid and distance measures see DRIVING on p.120.

Weight

grams	0	100	200	300	400	500	600	700	800	900	1 kg
ounces	0		4		8		12	1 lb	20		24		28		2 lb	

Temperature

| °C | -30 | -25 | -20 | -15 | -10 | -5 | 0 | 5 | 10 | 15 | 20 | 25 | 30 | 35 | 40 | 45 |
| °F | | -20 | -10 | 0 | 10 | 20 | 30 | 40 | 50 | 60 | 70 | 80 | 90 | 100 | 110 |

Length

YOUTH HOSTELS

Thailand has a few youth hostels; refer to *Hostelling International* (published by the International Youth Federation). Bangkok also has a YMCA (27 Sathorn Road; tel. 287 1900) and a YWCA (13 Sathorn Road; tel. 286 1936). Many Bangkok hotels offer student discounts.

SOME USEFUL EXPRESSIONS

NUMBERS

one	**neuhng**	fifteen	**sip-har**
two	**sorng**	sixteen	**sip-hok**
three	**sarm**	seventeen	**sip-jeht**
four	**see**	eighteen	**sip-(b)pairt**
five	**har**	nineteen	**sip-gow**
six	**hok**	twenty	**yee-sip**
seven	**jeht**	thirty	**sarm-sip**
eight	**(b)pairt**	forty	**see-sip**
nine	**gow**	fifty	**har-sip**
ten	**sip**	sixty	**hok-sip**
eleven	**sip-eht**	seventy	**jeht-sip**
twelve	**sip-sorng**	eighty	**(b)pairt-sip**
thirteen	**sip-sarm**	ninety	**gow-sip**
fourteen	**sip-see**	hundred	**roy**

DAYS OF THE WEEK

Sunday	**wan ar tit**	Thursday	**wan pa ru hat**
Monday	**wan jan**	Friday	**wan suk**
Tuesday	**wan ang karn**	Saturday	**wan sow**
Wednesday	**wan put**		

yesterday/today/tomorrow	**mua wan ni/wan ni/prung ni**
day/week/month/year	**wan/sap da/duan/pi**
left/right	**sai/khwa**
up/down	**bon/lang**
good/bad	**dee/lehw**
big/small	**yai/lehk**
cheap/expensive	**took/pairng**
hot/cold	**rorn/yehn**
old/new	**gow/mai**
early/late	**chow/sai**
easy/difficult	**ngai/yark**
heavy/light	**nak/bow**
here/there	**tee nee/tee nan**
next/last	**nar/tee laiw**
quick/slow	**rehw/char**
When does ... open/close?	**... pert/pit meua rai?**
What's the fare to ...?	**(b)pai ... kit tow rai?**
Could you speak more slowly?	**poot char long noy day mai?**

Index

Where an entry is referred to more than once, the main one is in **bold**.

144